ISLINGTON LIBRARIES
3 0120 008535

D1179052

Islington
Libraries

VICTORIAN BRITAIN THROUGH THE MAGIC LANTERN

VICTORIAN BRITAIN THROUGH THE MAGIC LANTERN

STEVE HUMPHRIES

SIDGWICK & JACKSON
London

To Anita from Doug

A silver spear of dancing dust spreads a picture on the wall;
The audience doesn't make a sound and as usual it's quite small;
But their eyes are bright as they watch the light,
And I feel their quiet awe,
The Lantern Girl weaves her magic spell,
In the darkness of the hall.

Title page: *A lantern image of commuter traffic arriving into central London over Waterloo Bridge,* c. *1880. Most Victorians walked to work or caught the horse bus*

Half-title: *Scene from 'The Rat Swallower',* c. *1875, a very popular comic sequence in magic lantern shows*

First published in Great Britain in 1989
by Sidgwick & Jackson Limited

Designed by Michael Head

ISBN 0-283-99900-4

Photoset by Rowland Phototypesetting Limited
Bury St Edmunds, Suffolk
Printed in England by
The Bath Press Limited, Bath
for Sidgwick & Jackson Limited
1 Tavistock Chambers, Bloomsbury Way
London WC1A 2SG

CONTENTS

ACKNOWLEDGEMENTS

We would like to thank all the people who have, in one way or another, helped us to put this book together. For help with information on the history of the magic lantern thanks to Em Kirkpatrick, Debbie Brown of Pollock's Toy Museum, David Francis of The Museum of the Moving Image, Ron Morris, Mike Smith, David Henry, Mervyn Heard, Jane Helliwell of Huddersfield Local Studies Library and James Belsey of the *Bristol Evening Post.* Thanks to everyone interviewed for their memories of the magic lantern, especially Ted Harrison and Doris Bailey. Special thanks are due to Lester Smith and to David and Eunice Elsbury who kindly allowed us to reproduce slides from their collections in this book. From Lester Smith we have used Polytechnic slides and pictures of slum life and mining, and we have drawn on the Elsbury's extensive collection of temperance and religious slides. Finally, thanks to Carey Smith of Sidgwick and Jackson who had the original idea for this book.

INTRODUCTION

FANTASTIC JUNK

Back in the nineteen-sixties it was practially impossible to go into an antique shop, a junk shop or even a jumble sale without seeing a shabby box of magic lantern slides for sale. Some were the once-treasured collections of grandparents who had just died. Others were the relics of old Sunday School classes. A few, like the 'Life in Many Lands' series, were long ago used as teaching aids. Most were practically worthless. Whole sets could be bought for just a few shillings. In fact many families simply dumped boxes of lantern slides into their dustbins to make way for all the gadgetry of the twentieth century. The magic lantern seemed to have no place in the new affluent and high-tech world of colour television and home movies.

Two of the first people to rediscover the value and beauty of these lantern slides were Doug and Anita Lear, then students of graphic design. They began touring junk shops all over Britain buying up boxes of slides and salvaging ancient magic lanterns which they would restore to their days of brass and mahogany glory. With the help of some rare instruction manuals for Victorian lantern operators they began staging shows to amuse friends. By now their idea of permanently reviving this long-dead art form was turning into an obsession. In 1976 they gave up their jobs and sold their home to start a new life running what was then the only professional lantern show in the world. The extraordinary nature of this venture was heightened by the fact that their show was staged on a narrowboat on the Grand Union Canal. The Lears converted half of the boat into a miniature Victorian-style theatre and the other into a home for their family. Called 'Phantasmagoria' after one of the first magic lantern entertainments in the 1800s, the show gave audiences a taste of the power and mystery of the Victorian lantern performance. The slide show usually included the eruption of Mount Vesuvius, a 'storm at sea', a sleeping man swallowing rats and a geometric 'chromatrope' (see colour section) sequence which pulsed and throbbed like a psychedelic light show. The images were accompanied by harmonium music, duck calls and a dizzy succession of bells, cymbals, kazoos, sirens and triangles, all played by Doug Lear.

This book features the Lears' unique collection of lantern slides, published here for the first time. Since their passion for lanterns began more than twenty years ago they have unearthed and restored some ten thousand photographic and painted slides, a further two thousand mechanical-effect slides and forty magic lanterns, making theirs one of the largest

Preceding page: *Doug and Anita Lear and son Elwyn on their narrowboat,* Magic Lantern, *on which they began staging magic lantern shows in 1976. Doug and Anita were two of the first people to rediscover the value and beauty of lantern slides and the pictures in this book are drawn from their collection, one of the largest of its kind in Britain*

collections of its type in Britain. The images range from rare documentary photographs of Irish peasants and Lancashire street urchins to early comic cartoons like the waiters who suddenly sprout pig's heads. Through these obscure and extraordinary images we are given a glimpse of the Victorian and Edwardian world as it must have looked to those who lived in it. And we are given many fascinating insights into the Victorian way of life.

Many middle-class children had their own toy lanterns to watch fairy tales and adventure stories in the nursery. But the first taste of the magic lantern came for the majority at Sunday School or Band of Hope meetings where Bible stories and moral fables were spelt out in melodramatic picture shows. Especially popular was the travelogue through which people who rarely ventured outside their home town or village were thrilled by views of cities and countries that they could never hope to visit.

The mass-produced lantern slides of Victorian and Edwardian Britain mirror the passions and prejudices of the age. Imperialism, for example, is brought into sharp focus through a host of pictures of wars, patriotic ceremonial and flag-waving processions. Lanternists – like today's press photographers – covered disasters, royal occasions and sporting triumphs, but communication was often so slow and difficult that some audiences saw these events months or years after they happened. There were advertisements, too, strangely primitive in their look and message, which punctuated many lantern shows.

The most beautiful lantern images are undoubtedly those produced in colour through the lost art of hand painting on glass slides. But perhaps the magic lantern was most interesting when it explored the social realities of Victorian life. Some lanternists, in the tradition of the early documentary photographers, tried to capture everyday life in the street, at work and at play. A few ventured into the slums. The unusual choice of subject and the sharpness of detail in many of these documentary pictures provide us with fascinating glimpses of everyday life a hundred years ago. The heyday of the lantern was in the 1880s and 1890s when magic lanterns were almost as common in middle-class homes as television sets are today. Such was the popularity of the lantern that a Lantern Society was formed and between 1889 and 1902 it published a magazine, *The Optical Magic Lantern Journal*. But the introduction of moving pictures and the cinema around the turn of the century marked the beginning of the end for the lantern. By the 1920s a once great and thriving industry was virtually dead.

A collection like that of the Lears would be practically impossible to build up today. With the fashion for Victoriana since the late sixties, the most interesting magic lantern slides have become 'collector's items' and their value has spiralled, especially in the last ten years. Boxes of painted and animated slides which used to be almost given away are now sold at Christie's and specialist auctions for hundreds or occasionally thousands of pounds. Members of the Magic Lantern Society of Great Britain, formed in 1976 and now flourishing with several hundred members – most of them avid collectors – are often the ones bidding the highest prices.

The Lears still perform magic lantern shows all over Europe, but no longer in the canal narrowboat. Their collection is now housed in the magic lantern museum they have opened at their new home in Morfa Nefyn in North Wales. This book is a testament to their extraordinary collection, and to the power of the magic lantern to illuminate the Victorian way of life.

CHAPTER ONE

VICTORIAN MAGIC

In 1890 the Chairman of the Lantern Society recalled how his fascination with lanterns had begun some forty years earlier when, as a child, he saw a show in his village school at Wixhall, Shropshire.

Preceding page: *Queen Victoria and Prince Albert, a hand-tinted photographic lantern slide,* c. *1855. During Victoria's reign the magic lantern grew from an obscure novelty into one of the most popular entertainments of the age*

> Such a crowd. All the blankets and bedquilts in the neighbourhood were used in darkening the innumerable windows of the schoolroom, which was a very large room, capable of holding some hundreds. The falling snow, Babes in the Wood, all these things paled before the final climax – the man swallowing rats. With the other boys I started counting but I shall never muster up the courage to tell your readers how many rats that man ate. It was very wonderful. I always had a curiosity about the lantern after that day.

The rat swallower was the most popular lantern sequence of all time. If an audience had never seen it before, their excitement at this primitive cartoon could literally bring the house down. One pioneer lanternist described his first-ever lantern show in a village hall in the 1850s.

A magic lantern show given to poor and destitute children by the Fulham Liberal Club in London, 1889. The 'rat swallower' was the most popular lantern sequence of all time

A drawing by Gavarni, published in 1801, shows an itinerant lantern showman of the time. Strapped to his back is his small tin lantern – which would only have projected a distance of around three metres – and his collection of painted slides. His appearance vividly portrays the hard life endured by the early 'galantee' entertainers, who would walk from one town or village to another staging their shows

The first picture was projected on the screen. This if I remember right was a man swallowing rats. This caused a stomping and shouting such as would eclipse a more civilized audience and made the beams of the floor spring and as luck would have it the screen framework fell over towards the lantern. And crash – the frame knocked the lens out of the flange and the lantern over. After peace was restored and the audience dismissed I examined the apparatus and concluded that the five shillings I received hardly compensated for a broken condenser and a dented lens mount.

A unique silk poster, advertising a magic lantern gala in Devon, 1844. This poster was found in the bottom of a box in a Kensington antique shop in 1972, stuck together in a tight ball with only the word 'dissolving' visible, and it took Anita Lear several weeks to disentangle the hand-stitched silk fibre from the wood glue plastered all over the poster. Tickets for Mr Gyngell's show at 1/6 (7½p) represented about a week's wages for a North Devonshire farm worker at the time. The audience for more expensive and sophisticated lantern shows like this were drawn from the ranks of the well-to-do and the middle classes

The story of the magic lantern begins in Germany in the mid-seventeenth century. It was first described in 1671 in a book, *Ars Magna Lucis et Umbrae*, written by a Jesuit priest and scientist, Athanasius Kircher. But no one knows whether Kircher actually invented it. The first lanterns used a simple oil lamp and lens to project and enlarge glass paintings. This breakthrough in the field of optics was the culmination of centuries of experimentation, often to create supernatural images. Magician priests in the ancient civilizations of China, Greece and Rome had used mirrors to summon up spectral figures at religious rituals and festivals. Father Kircher was one of the last priests to openly concern himself with optics. After him the art of projection became more closely connected with entertainment than with religion. Samuel Pepys recorded in his diary that he bought a lantern on 22 August 1666 and found it greatly amusing, describing it as 'the lanthorne that shews tricks'.

For a hundred and fifty years the magic lantern was left largely in the hands of travelling small-time entertainers. With their bulky lanterns strapped to their backs, and often accompanied by a hurdy-gurdy player, they would tramp from one village or town to another. On arrival they would announce that the 'galantee show' was in town. The term 'galantee show' derived from the cry of foreign showmen (many itinerant lanternists were Italian) who shouted 'Galante so!', 'galante' being their word for fine and 'so' their pronunciation of 'show'.

These travelling entertainers would perform in private homes, showing slides that combined the grotesque, the religious and the humorous. One popular early slide was 'Pull Devil, Pull Baker' which portrayed the last judgement upon a baker who sold bread short of weight and was carried off to hell in his own basket. They usually showed the same hand-painted slide sequences year after year, so they were careful not to return to the same town or village too often.

However, the magic lantern emerged from obscurity around the beginning of the nineteenth century when entertainers began captivating audiences with lantern spectacles called 'Phantasmagoria'. Hidden behind a semi-transparent sheet with simple lanterns, these showmen used the 'magic' powers of their projector to conjure up what seemed to be spectres of the dead. The Phantasmagoria were the idea of a Belgian, Etienne Gaspard Robert (often known as Robertson) and were first staged in Paris. They were popularized in Britain by Paul de

*An engraving by the satirist James Gillray, published in 1792, depicts the reception of the emissaries of King George III at the court of the Chinese Emperor in Peking. Among the gifts of children's toys is a miniature magic lantern (*centre bottom*). Its inclusion indicates its novelty value at this time*

'The magic lantern', a drawing by Phiz which appeared in The London Illustrated Times *in December 1858. By mid-century the lantern show was increasingly considered to be an instructive and entertaining diversion for genteel young minds. More and more middle-class parents bought lanterns for use at home and staged shows for their children in the drawing-room and the nursery*

Two pages from the 1892 catalogue of Archer and Sons, one of the leading producers of magic lanterns and lantern slides. By the 1890s the catalogue of this Liverpool company had grown to over 300 pages. Its success mirrored the remarkable popularity of the magic lantern in late Victorian Britain. The catalogue boasted that the public could choose from 'considerably over 1,300 different sets' either for sale or hire. Some were 'rackwork' mechanical slides through which an illusion of movement could be created. Circular movements could be made by turning a long lever connected to a brass-toothed cog running around the edge of the rackwork slide. Customers could also choose from hundreds of lanterns ranging from cheap toy ones selling for a few shillings to elaborate triunials priced at anything between ten and fifty guineas. Public lecturers also advertised through the pages of the catalogue. In 1892 a lecturer complete with 'superior limelight dissolving view lanterns' could be hired for £2 2s (£2. 10) a performance

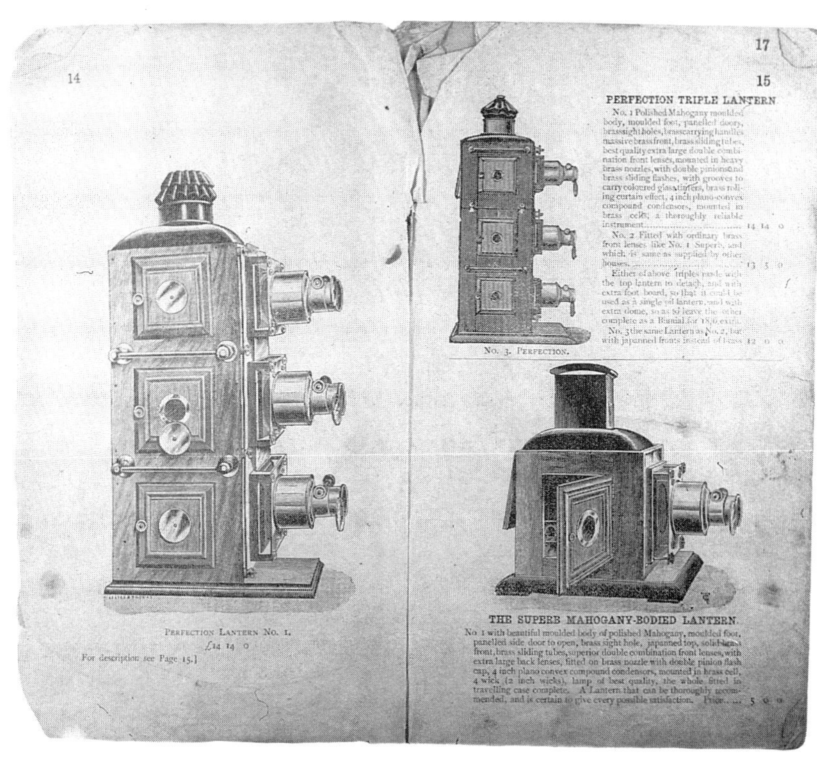

14

PERFECTION LANTERN No. 1,
£14 14 0
For description see Page 15.]

17

15

PERFECTION TRIPLE LANTERN

No. 1 Polished Mahogany moulded body, moulded foot, panelled doors, brass sight holes, brass carrying handles massive brass front, brass sliding tubes, best quality extra large double combination front lenses, mounted in heavy brass nozzles, with double pinions and brass sliding flashes, with grooves to carry coloured glass tinters, brass rolling curtain effect, 4 inch plano-convex compound condensors, mounted in brass cells, a thoroughly reliable instrument.............................. 14 14 0

No. 2 Fitted with ordinary brass front lenses like No. 1 Superb, and which is same as supplied by other houses.............................. 13 5 0

Either of above triples made with the top lantern to detach, and with extra foot board, so that it could be used as a single oil lantern, and with extra dome, so as to leave the other complete as a Biunial for 18/6 extra.

No. 3 the same Lantern as No. 2, but with japanned fronts instead of brass 12 0 0

No. 3. PERFECTION.

THE SUPERB MAHOGANY-BODIED LANTERN.

No 1 with beautiful moulded body of polished Mahogany, moulded foot, panelled side door to open, brass sight hole, japanned top, solid brass front, brass sliding tubes, superior double combination front lenses, with extra large back lenses, fitted on brass nozzle with double pinion flash cap, 4 inch plano convex compound condensors, mounted in brass cell, 4 wick (2 inch wicks), lamp of best quality, the whole fitted in travelling case complete. A Lantern that can be thoroughly recommended, and is certain to give every possible satisfaction. Price...... 5 0 0

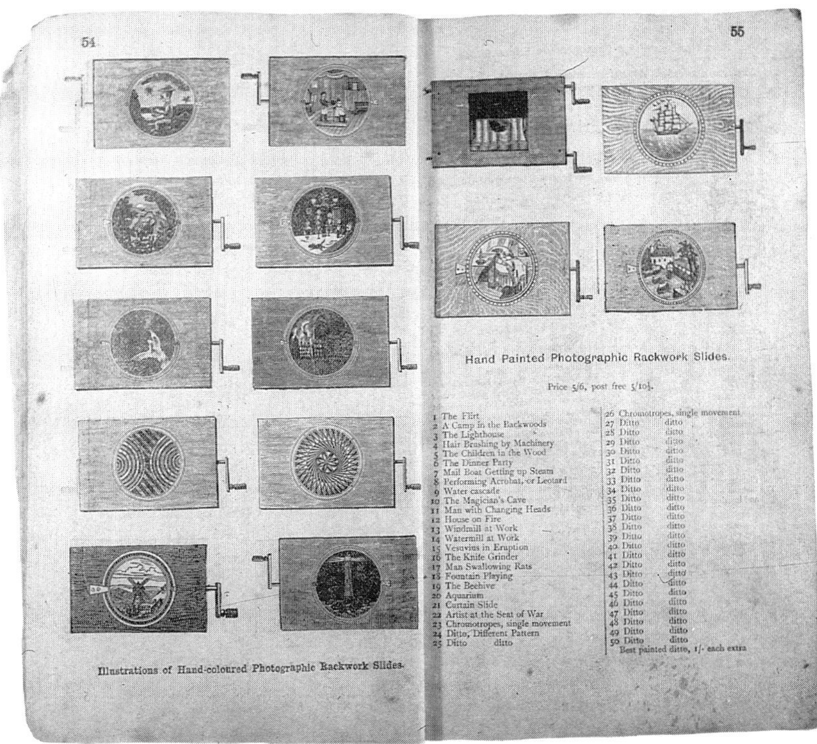

54

55

Illustrations of Hand-coloured Photographic Rackwork Slides.

Hand Painted Photographic Rackwork Slides.

Price 5/6, post free 5/10½.

1 The Flirt
2 A Camp in the Backwoods
3 The Lighthouse
4 Hair Brushing by Machinery
5 The Children in the Wood
6 The Dinner Party
7 Mail Boat Getting up Steam
8 Performing Acrobat, or Leotard
9 Water cascade
10 The Magician's Cave
11 Man with Changing Heads
12 House on Fire
13 Windmill at Work
14 Watermill at Work
15 Vesuvius in Eruption
16 The Knife Grinder
17 Man Swallowing Rats
18 Fountain Playing
19 The Beehive
20 Aquarium
21 Curtain Slide
22 Artist at the Seat of War
23 Chromotropes, single movement
24 Ditto, Different Pattern
25 Ditto ditto
26 Chromotropes, single movement
27 Ditto ditto
28 Ditto ditto
29 Ditto ditto
30 Ditto ditto
31 Ditto ditto
32 Ditto ditto
33 Ditto ditto
34 Ditto ditto
35 Ditto ditto
36 Ditto ditto
37 Ditto ditto
38 Ditto ditto
39 Ditto ditto
40 Ditto ditto
41 Ditto ditto
42 Ditto ditto
43 Ditto ditto
44 Ditto ditto
45 Ditto ditto
46 Ditto ditto
47 Ditto ditto
48 Ditto ditto
49 Ditto ditto
50 Ditto ditto
Best painted ditto, 1/- each extra

Philipstal in London and Edinburgh in the 1800s. The scientist Sir David Brewster described what happened at them:

> The small theatre of exhibition was lighted only by one hanging lamp, the flame of which was drawn up into an opaque chimney or shade when the performance began. In this semi-obscurity the curtain rose and displayed a cave with skeletons and other terrific figures in relief upon its walls. The flickering light was then drawn up beneath its shroud, and the spectators, left in total darkness, found themselves in the midst of thunder and lightning. A thin transparent screen had, unknown to the spectators, been let down after the disappearance of the light, and upon it the flashes of lightning and all the subsequent appearances were represented. The thunder and lightning were followed by the figures of ghosts, skeletons, and known individuals whose eyes and mouths were made to move by the shifting of combined slides. After the first figure had been exhibited for a short time, it began to grow less and less, as if removed to a great distance, and at last vanished in a small cloud of light. Out of this same cloud another figure began to appear and gradually grew larger and larger and approached the spectator until it attained its perfect development.

These were the Hammer horror films of the day and people would come from miles around to witness them. Sometimes a curtain of smoke was used instead of a screen. Spectacles like these could be especially terrifying for sensitive children. Harriet Martineau, the popular Victorian writer, remembered how 'at the age of thirteen when I was pretending to take care of little children during the exhibition, I could never look at it without having the back of the chair to grasp, or hurting myself to carry off the intolerable sensation . . . it was so like my nightmare dreams that I shrieked aloud'. The Phantasmagoria went out of fashion by the late 1820s, but the use of the lantern for magical and supernatural effects was to continue in the theatre where it became an essential piece of equipment.

During the Victorian period the magic lantern was to broaden its appeal to all sections of society, becoming one of the most popular and respectable entertainments of the age. This growing popularity was closely linked with a series of inventions which made the lantern much more sophisticated. First

Scene from Robertson's 'Phantasmagoria', c. 1800. Behind the screen, unseen by the audience, is a moving magic lantern which projects a terrifying sequence of skulls, skeletons and monsters. These were the 'horror films' of the day and attracted huge audiences

'Exhibition of a Democratic Transparency', an engraving by James Gillray published in 1799. The Phantasmagoria with its 'secret' back projection had by this time clearly become familiar enough to the public to be used in political satire. The caption reads, 'Representing the secret committee throwing a light upon the dark sketches of a Revolution found among the papers of the Jacobin Societies lately apprehended'. A House of Commons committee is 'illuminating' the fact that the troublemakers' real intention is revolution, as had occurred ten years earlier in France. Irish politicians of the day shy away from the terrible images brightly lit in the dark chamber

One of the only drawings of an outdoor lantern show. In it the lanternist summons up a grotesque devil of the type that featured in the Phantasmagoria. The supposed power of these 'evil images' to corrupt children and young people (who always formed a sizeable portion of the audiences) was a source of great concern to contemporary moralists

came the development of dissolving views in the late 1830s, pioneered by Henry Langdon Childe who had served his apprenticeship to the lantern on Phantasmagoria shows. By placing two lanterns side by side and projecting their images out onto the same point he found it was possible to dissolve one view into another so that as one picture faded away another took its place. This was quickly followed by the discovery of what came to be called 'dioramic dissolves'. Audiences were thrilled by the spectacle of day turning into night, or winter into summer by dissolving two views of the same scene at different times of the day or during different seasons. Dissolving views were to become synonymous with magic lantern entertainments. One of the most prized skills of the lanternist was the ability to orchestrate these 'dissolves' so smoothly that one image melted imperceptibly into another – a sight of great beauty. The achievement of these smooth transitions was made easier by the development of two-in-one ('biunial') or three-in-one ('triunial') lanterns. These were two or three lanterns joined one on top of the other, with two or three lenses and lights. These brass and mahogany monsters were the state of the art for the Victorian professional showman, the Rolls-Royces of the lantern world.

Equally important in the growing popularity of the magic lantern was the development of an effective source of light, and thus of a sharp image. Until the early nineteenth century, lanterns had been illuminated with oil lamps, which were too weak to throw images any distance onto big screens. However, in the early Victorian years the discovery of limelight – used at first for theatre spotlights – transformed the magic lantern. Limelight was produced by a flame of oxygen and hydrogen gases under pressure impinging on a cylinder of lime which, when hot, provided an intense, brilliant light. Now the lantern could project sharp pictures onto large screens, entertaining larger audiences.

The most spectacular limelight shows or exhibitions were staged at London's Royal Polytechnic Institution in Regent Street, described at the time as 'a temple of science, art and magic'. It was opened in 1838 and for the next forty years provided a vast programme of popular education and entertainment, much of which revolved round the magic lantern. The Royal Polytechnic, which charged an admission fee of a

'The Corsican Brothers', c. 1880, part of a set of twenty-four hand-painted slides based on a Victorian playlet often performed in toy theatres. It tells the story of two brothers, one of whom is killed in a duel between them and returns as a ghost. The top slide is the forest glade where the duel takes place; the bottom one is superimposed on it through a mechanical effect which flashes the different actions onto the picture in a series of jerky movements. This was the closest mid-Victorian audiences got to moving pictures

shilling, was one of London's great tourist attractions and played a key role in popularizing the magic lantern in Victorian Britain. Audiences of thousands thrilled to the Polytechnic's famous dissolving views projected onto its giant screen by Henry Childe. The art of magic lantern projection reached its peak at the Polytechnic and its shows were reported in newspapers alongside opera and theatre reviews. The shows ranged from travel lectures to astronomy to current affairs. Often banks of lanterns would be used to create special effects.

Limelight shows, however, could be lethal. The mixture of hydrogen and oxygen which made limelight was potentially explosive and occasionally there were gruesome accidents. Limelight was certainly too dangerous for home use, and domestic lanterns continued to use small oil lamps. From time to time lanterns exploded during exhibitions, causing disastrous fires. More commonly, the rubber bags or metal cylinders carrying compressed gases exploded as they were conveyed to magic lantern events around Britain – usually as a result of being mishandled or accidentally dropped by railway staff. There were so many injuries or deaths that several railway companies banned gas cylinders from passenger trains. To avoid detection, lantern lecturers concealed their cylinders in cricket bags or instrument cases. The best-known, like the Royal Polytechnic lecturers who travelled round the country giving lantern shows, would be searched on stations, so they would secretly parcel up their equipment and send it in disguise ahead of them. Other gases like ether vapour and acetylene were experimented with, but they proved equally perilous. The problem was only fully solved with the coming of electricity around the turn of the century, when the many limelight lanterns were converted to make use of Edison's new incandescent bulb.

Another important factor which greatly increased the popularity and versatility of the magic lantern was the development of mechanical slides. Before the Victorian period slides were usually glass plates without any moving parts or long strips which were slowly pulled behind the lens to tell a story, one image after another. But from the 1830s onwards the quest for the magic of moving pictures led to the invention of a variety of trick slides which appeared quite miraculous at the time. These mechanical slides – known as slipping, lever, pulley and rackwork slides – had moving parts, operated by hand. They were very simple in design but added a fantastic

A 'pagoda' magic lantern, c. 1900. Ornamental lanterns with elaborate, often exotic, designs were popular in Victorian times – an age when lanterns would be proudly displayed in the middle-class drawing-room. Now, however, there are only a few lanterns like this remaining and they are highly prized by collectors

range to the lanternist's repertoire. The lanternist could now make a ship sink in a thunderstorm, speed a train across a railway bridge, turn the sails of a windmill, recreate battles on land and at sea, or engulf a factory with fire. In one of the Royal Polytechnic's popular presentations, 'The Siege of Delhi', several lanterns simulated artillery fire, shells bursting and the carnage of war. The show was described by John Pepper, the Polytechnic's principal lecturer: 'The optical effects were assisted by various sounds in imitation of war's alarms, for the production of which more volunteers than were absolutely required would occasionally trespass behind the scenes, and produce those terrific sounds that some persons of a nervous temperament said were really stunning.'

Perhaps the most sensational of all these special effects was the chromatrope – another of the inventions of Henry Langdon Childe – which created a 'kaleidoscope' of geometric shapes that appeared to pull the spectator into its whirling vortex. 'Artificial firework displays', as they were often called, were an unforgettable experience for many Victorian audiences. It was a special effect that was to remain immensely popular in lantern shows until the end of the century.

A small biunial (double-lensed) lantern only 65 cm high, dating from the 1880s. The two lenses made possible 'dissolving views', for which the magic lantern became famous. Though these machines were mass produced during the late Victorian period, today they are quite rare. Many thousands of lanterns were handed into the government during the munitions drives of the two world wars and their elaborate brass work melted down into bullets

The final key development which revolutionized the magic lantern was the invention of photography which began to be used to produce photographic glass slides from the 1850s onwards. Until then lantern slides had been hand-painted. Some were exquisitely beautiful, but these tended to be expensive. The majority were of rather poor quality and the paintings slapdash and unconvincing. The coming of photography made it possible to produce images which were sharper and which captured 'real life' in a way that was quite novel to Victorians. Photography vastly increased the range and attractiveness of the magic lantern show, adding a new dimension to the travelogue and making possible the hugely popular 'life model' genre in which actors posed in various settings to illustrate many moral and melodramatic stories. The development of photography did lead in the long run to the demise of hand-painted slides, which now seemed old-fashioned and unrealistic. But for most of the century photography complemented rather than competed with the magic lantern show, because it was still not technically possible to print photographs in newspapers and they were rarely used in books. Although studio, portrait photography developed quite early on, the most likely place an 'ordinary' person could expect to see a non-studio photograph was at a magic lantern show.

The growing popularity of the magic lantern in mid-Victorian times meant that it was potentially big business and hundreds of manufacturers sprouted up all over Britain mass-producing lantern slides in the new standard format of 3¼″ square. The range of slides was staggering, covering everything from fairy tales to literary classics and from travelogues to temperance lectures. The largest lantern slide factory was that established in the 1870s by the Bamforth family in the small West Yorkshire town of Holmfirth. Ten years later there were twenty-eight firms who manufactured lanterns and slides in London alone. Two of the largest companies in the capital, Walter Tyler and W. C. Hughes, both boasted exhibition galleries where thousands of glasses were on view. These could be examined by prospective purchasers through special viewers like those used today for looking at colour transparencies.

The 1880s and 1890s were the heyday of the magic lantern. A host of amateur and professional showmen staged lantern entertainments all over Britain. Often they were 'for one night only' and an admission fee of around sixpence would be collected at the door. There were daily lantern shows at the Crystal Palace. The most spectacular professional shows might involve eight projectionists and attract up to two thousand people. Lantern slides were also used extensively to illustrate educational and scientific lectures in Mechanics' Institutes, learned societies, museums and universities. On top of this, many organizations like churches and temperance societies staged regular lantern shows to spread their propaganda. And owning a lantern for home use, and a toy lantern for the children, became a feature of middle-class life. To be able to put on a good show at Christmas or during the dark winter evenings came to be seen as an essential mark of status and fashionability amongst better-off families.

The world of the magic lantern had been transformed since

the days when it was dominated by poor itinerant showmen who tramped from village to village with a few slides to show. Yet such was the popularity of lantern entertainments that even in the 1900s a few street-wise showmen could scratch a living giving open-air shows to working-class audiences who could not afford to see a lantern entertainment anywhere else. In 1901 *The Optical and Magic Lantern Journal* reported on a portable, 'horse drawn' street entertainment for several hundred people in 'a town in the North of England':

> A waggon was drawn up close to the kerbstone, the back part facing the crowd; it was covered square fashion with tarpaulin. A white sheet was fixed at the back and humorous slides were being thrown on it in quick succession. During the progress of the exhibition, which lasted about twenty minutes, collections were made by two men, and judging from the repeated chink, chink of the coppers as they fell into the boxes, the receipts must have been large.

In the closing years of Victoria's reign the magic lantern seemed to have a secure future. There was apprehension at the growing competition from moving pictures and the cinema, but in the late 1890s this new art was still in its infancy, dogged by technical problems and incapable of the smoothness and majesty of a magic lantern show. To some lanternists, the cinematograph was just a passing fashion. A much more important debate amongst the professional lanternists of the time was how to extend the 'lantern season' from its traditional highpoint around Christmas and the winter months to the spring and summer. The magic lantern show had become so much part of the fabric of the Victorian way of life, they just could not imagine a world without it.

'The water mill', a beautiful hand-painted dissolving view, c. *1860. Winter* (top) *slowly melts into summer* (below). *In addition, the figures walk up the path and through the cottage door, an effect achieved by 'slipping glasses'. Dissolving views typically looked back to an idyllic pre-industrial past far away from the smoky world of railways and factories created in the Victorian age*

Left and opposite: *Two 'snapshots' of Bank Holiday scenes on Hampstead Heath illustrate the increasing use of documentary images in magic lantern shows in the 1890s. In the pre-motor car age many thousands of Londoners – especially poorer people – spent their Bank Holidays on Hampstead Heath where there were many activities to be enjoyed for free. Skipping with the big rope was in late Victorian times a game enjoyed by adults as well as children, while* (opposite) *peering through the telescope was then a novel amusement*

Seaside resorts were popular subjects for magic lantern travelogue sequences. The deceptively modern-looking pleasure park at Southport was pictured in 1898. It hugged the beach and the shoreline, providing all the fun of the fair for northern working-class visitors. Other parts of Southport, like the Lord Street area, retained the traditional elegance of an old watering-place, appealing strongly to more 'refined' and monied holidaymakers

London appeared more often in lantern travelogue sets than any other city. The scenes of daily life in 'the heart of the Empire' must have been fascinating to the many members of lantern audiences who had never visited the capital

CHAPTER TWO

TOYS AND TREATS

In 1890 Christopher Rendle, a well-known lanternist of his day, described the beginning of his lifelong fascination with the magic lantern in an article, 'Christmastide Reminiscences', published in *The Optical Magic Lantern Journal*.

> The first lantern experience I can remember dates from the Christmas evening of 1860. I was a boy at school. It was a severe winter. Our little cottage in the north of England was enveloped by hoar-frost. Uncle Bob had brought us about a month previously a book of a real pantomime and promised to paint some pictures to illustrate the dialogue with his magic lantern if we could undertake to study the parts. (The pantomime was 'The Wild Man and The Gorilla'.) The rehearsals were enthusiastic. There were a dozen pictures in all for this lengthy exhibition. Remember we had not the facilities for making a selection from a catalogue such as you see today, but glad to get what we could. The evening came, the lantern set up; the sheet across the kitchen. How we shouted with delight; we could not speak our lines for laughing; the part singing was impeded with an occasional ripple; and Uncle Bob (who played the gorilla) could not groan for the hilarity underneath his waistcoat.

This was a fairly typical initiation into the world of the magic lantern for a child in mid-Victorian Britain. The lantern was the latest fashion in home entertainments amongst the middle classes. It would be brought out by father to amuse the children on dark winter evenings and most of all at Christmas. On Christmas Day – the great festival of the family, essentially created by the Victorians – there would be games like Blind Man's Buff, Hunt the Slipper and Musical Chairs, but the day would often culminate in a grand magic lantern show.

This tradition of magic lantern shows in the winter months and particularly around Christmas went back to the eighteenth century. For many years travelling or 'galantee' showmen had put on shows in the houses of 'gentlefolk'. But by the 1850s and 60s when the mass production of lanterns was getting underway, better off fathers could buy their own equipment and stage their own parlour or nursery shows. With this change, the old ghostly and grotesque images which were the stock in trade of the showmen gave way to more domesticated

Preceding page: *'Mrs Punch' or 'Judy', a hand-painted slipping slide much loved by children,* c. *1850. The nose grows as the slipping glass is slowly moved*

Home for Little Boys,
NEAR FARNINGHAM, KENT.

Cottage Homes for 350 Homeless Little Ones.

Admit the Bearer to
AN EVENING ASSEMBLY
in the
FESTIVAL CONCERT ROOMS,
YORK,
On Tuesday, 25th October, 1881,
when
THE MILITARY BAND
of the Home, consisting of [illegible] Performers,
WILL PLAY OVERTURES, SELECTIONS, AND MARCHES,
and
DISSOLVING VIEWS
will be exhibited, illustrating
The Story of the Little Boys,
With Descriptive Lecture by the
Rev. H. J. BERGUER, M.A., Vicar of St. Philip's, Islington.
The Boys of the Band will also sing several
Choruses and Part Songs.

The Chair will be taken at half-past seven o'clock by
Dr. Shann, J.P.

London Offices— A. O. CHARLES,
Ludgate Circus. *Secretary.*

Programme for a lantern concert for orphans in October 1881. For children in institutions the magic lantern show was one of the great treats of the year. It was usually staged during the winter months, especially at Christmas

slide shows thought appropriate for children, like moral tales and fairy stories. This put some of the old showmen out of business. One told social investigator Henry Mayhew, 'the galantee show don't answer now because magic lanterns is so cheap in the shops. When we started they wasn't so common. It was a reglar thing for Christmas, the Galantee show. But we can't keep hold of a good thing in these times.'

The magic lantern was one of a host of optical toys that were developed in the nineteenth century. This abundance of new optical inventions reflected the scientific achievement and progress of the Victorian age and a keenness to turn it into profit. One of the earliest optical toys was the kaleidoscope, a tube containing two long mirrors, the end of which held small pieces of coloured glass. When it was shaken it produced a

A child's 'educational' slide produced in 1900 by German Ernest Plank's magic lantern factory in Nuremberg, which exported thousands of slide sets all over the world every year. This circular slide entitled 'The Human Races' illustrates eight racial stereotypes. The images graphically portray late Victorian racist thinking: it was assumed at the time that the Europeans were a superior breed. It is revealing that the title chosen was 'The Human Races' as opposed to 'The Human Race'

series of brilliant abstract patterns like a mosaic. Many children found the kaleidoscope intriguing, but even more popular was the stereoscope invented by Sir Charles Wheatstone in 1832. When seen through the stereoscope eyepiece, pictures took on a striking third dimension. Views of the Taj Mahal and the Pyramids looked more 'real', enthralling many children. Then there were portable dioramas which created topographical illusions fascinating to adults and children alike. One country girl visiting her more sophisticated cousins in London at Christmas in the 1830s was amazed by their diorama. It had twelve coloured views of castles, abbeys and mountain scenery with transparent skies, and a second set of skies which, 'being placed behind those of the picture, were steadily unrolled by turning a handle and produced the most varied and beautiful effects on the scenery, which could thus at pleasure be illuminated gradually with sunshine or moonbeams'.

But by mid-Victorian times the magic lantern had established itself as the most popular optical toy for children. Among the first toy lanterns for children was that made by Auguste Lapierre, a French tinsmith living in Paris, in 1843. He was too poor to take his children to a magic lantern performance, so he made them one out of a can and a candle. His toy lanterns were so well received that he decided to go into production. The basic model was just a tin box containing a candle-holder, a concave mirror and a lens. Lapierre supplied the coloured glass slide strips, which children could project onto any plain white wall acting as a screen.

By the 1850s toy magic lanterns were being sold in their tens of thousands in toy shops in Britain, Europe and the United States. Most toy lanterns brought into Britain were imported from Germany, which dominated the early toy industry. The largest manufacturer of toy magic lanterns was Ernest Plank who by 1899 was turning out 150,000 a year from his Nurem-

A selection from a set of hand-painted 'grotesques', produced to entertain children in 1873. Though crudely painted in a 'primitive' style, the colours have great vivacity, especially when projected on to the screen

A postcard, c. *1900, which vividly illustrates the great enjoyment that Victorian children must have got from playing with their toy lanterns*

Below: *'The waiter and the Pig', a hand-painted, mechanical slipping slide,* c. *1870. The lanternist would 'slip' the glass slide quickly so that the waiter's and the pig's heads would be switched in a split second. Slipping slides like this made possible a host of surreal visual jokes which greatly appealed to Victorian children*

'Balancing the Ball', a slipping slide, c. *1890. Slide sets featuring circus artists, like clowns, jugglers, tumblers and acrobats, were great favourites among children. The simple movement made possible by the slipping slide gave the illusion that a 'trick' had been performed before the children's eyes*

Right: *A bronze toy lantern produced by the Lapierre factory in France in 1880. Many thousands of toy lanterns were imported into Britain in the nineteenth century from France and Germany, by virtue of the fact that they were much cheaper and generally better value than the lanterns produced here. They became one of the most popular Christmas presents for middle-class children, especially boys*

berg factory. The very cheapest miniature toy lantern sold for less than a shilling (5p). As late as 1913 it was possible to buy 'Our Boy's Lantern' together with three slides from Gamage's, the well-known London department store, for 10½d (4p). Yet even this small sum was often beyond the means of many working-class children who would have been lucky to get a halfpenny pocket money a week. One such child was Ted Harrison, brought up in Hoxton, one of the poorest parts of London, in the 1900s.

> I never had a toy lantern, we couldn't afford it, but there was a boy down the street who had one, they were a bit better off. And he used to hold magic lantern shows in the front passageway of their house. And we used to have to pay a marble or two sweets or perhaps even a halfpenny to see his slides. But it wasn't much good, it was only candle lit, so sometimes you could hardly see a thing.

Until this time the very cheapest toy lanterns still used candles which created faint flickering images. However, the market was dominated by more elaborate and expensive lanterns than these, for the magic lantern was essentially a middle-class toy. By the 1900s most used paraffin lamps, gas light, acetylene lamps or even electricity. Ornamental toy lanterns made of bronzed tin were immensely popular, and the finest specimens would be finished in steel, copper and brass, with lustrous colours. The grandest lanterns would be proudly displayed in the nursery or the drawing-room.

The range of slides available for children increased in tandem with the growing popularity of 'family' and 'toy' lanterns. To begin with, there were few slides to choose from, and most of them showed scenes with comic and grotesque characters like Punch and Harlequin. But by the 1880s children could choose from a growing range of slide sequences illustrating a mass of nursery rhymes or fairy tales. To broaden the choice of children, and to encourage new skills, children's annuals and magazines of the time like *The Boy's Own Paper* constantly gave advice to readers on how to make and paint their own slides. Slides were painted by placing a piece of glass over a design drawn on a sheet of paper and tracing the outlines in Indian ink. Fine detail could be scraped in with a needle-like tool. Colour was then added and the highlights were picked out with a needle point.

Opening title slide from a hand-painted set, illustrating the traditional nursery rhyme 'Old Mother Hubbard', c. 1875. The images are made even more bizarre by the strange period costumes of the characters

'The Improved Ordinance', a comic slide produced by the Wesleyan Methodist Sunday School Association in the 1880s. 'Jokes' like this one, which played on the supposed ignorance of African tribesmen and women, were very common in children's slides

'The Female Volunteer', part of a one-off home-made set of sixty hand-painted slides, c. 1850. The joke is, presumably, that the crinolined hoops are like a suit of armour. This set has an extraordinary history. Doug Lear bought them from a milkman in Plymouth who was himself given the slides by a family of destitute travellers as a way of settling an unpaid milk bill

But by the turn of the century the DIY tradition had practically disappeared as a result of the welter of choice offered by the big commercial manufacturers. In the 1900s, for example, the Christmas catalogues of the great emporiums like Gamage's in London were listing a staggering array of lantern slides which included classics like Alice in Wonderland and The Water Babies. Parents often bought the slides for their children, sometimes to be shown on father's 'superior' lantern, and manufacturers were not slow to produce educational and religious sets – complete with readings – designed to appeal to the Victorian concern with improving children's minds and morals. 'Views of Foreign parts', 'Religious Stories for Children' and 'Famous Pictures of the World' reproducing old masters, were all big sellers.

The growing awareness of the educational potential of the magic lantern led to demands for its introduction into the school classroom. Crusading lanternists argued that it should

'Bill Adams, The Hero of Waterloo', one of a set of thirteen hand-coloured slides produced in 1885. Bill Adams was a popular comic figure, especially among the young, in late Victorian times. Through the text which accompanied the slides, the yokel Bill tells tall stories – in the vernacular – in which he claims to have helped the 'heroes' of British history to their military triumphs. 'Well, then,' sez Nelson, 'there's only one man as I knows can take this 'ere job on.' 'Who's that?' sez the Dook (Wellington). 'Why, Bill Adams!' sez Nelson

be seen as something more than a toy and a treat for children, and that it could transform the teaching of subjects like history, geography, science and geology. A few pioneering teachers built up early 'visual aid' libraries based on photographs they took on holiday and pictures they cut from books. One Mr Church, for example, headteacher of Bath Road Board School in Bristol, spent twenty years building up a collection of 2,000 lantern slides on history, geography and zoology. And in London from the 1900s onwards the history of the capital was taught to senior pupils through a series of lantern slides. However, the idea that the lantern was an indulgence and an entertainment remained very strong, and its use was widely resisted by teachers and educationists. As a result the magic lantern show made little headway in the elementary schools of Victorian and Edwardian Britain. For the most part it was only used as a treat for younger pupils at Christmas or as a special reward for regular attendance and good behaviour.

'Jack the Giant Killer', a crude hand-painted one-off set, c. *1850. In it Jack slays a series of giants, one of whom has two heads. This tale is typical of the many frightening and gruesome stories used to entertain Victorian children*

'Hop O' My Thumb', an exquisite hand-painted lantern set, c. *1850. The traditional fairy tale is told of hero Hop, a tiny child, who steals the giant's boots and presents them to the King. Although this particular fairy tale is practically unknown today it would have been familiar to many Victorian children*

CHAPTER THREE

MORALS AND MODELS

Every Monday evening in the early years of the century Doris Bailey was one of hundreds of Bethnal Green children eager to see the Band of Hope magic lantern show in the local church hall in London's East End. In her book, *Children of the Green*, she recalls:

> It attracted so many children as to need two sittings. We would queue up for about three quarters of an hour, and the queue was so long by the time the doors opened that there would be another three hundred or so waiting to get in when we came out. Some of the children came out and tagged on to the end of the queue again, so much did they enjoy it. Yet it was a very simple meeting really. We sang cheerful hymns flashed on a big screen, lovely hymns about drinking pure water and not yielding to temptation. The top favourite appealed to me very much, the words had so much meaning for me.
>
> As on the path of life we tread,
> We come to many a place,
> Where if not careful we may fall, and sink into disgrace.
>
> There was a really rousing chorus which we yelled at the top of our voices.
>
> Don't step there, don't step there, don't step there,
> For if not careful you may fall, don't step there.
> The drinker's path is one beset with many a hidden snare,
> Oh, shun the drink shop's fatal spell, I warn you,
> Don't step there.
>
> After the hymns the lights were lowered and we had a story, illustrated by Magic Lantern slides. A deep hush settled over us as we listened to the lovely stories. Nearly always about poor children living in hovels whose fathers drank away every penny. My dad was a saint compared with these fathers. How we all wept when father stole the blankets off the children's bed to take to the pawnshop for drink money. And we sobbed audibly when mother walked the streets in the snow to get help for her sick baby, clasped to her breast for warmth, while dad lay in a drunken stupor on the bare boarded floor. Then, the minister or the vicar met up with the family, and when the dog collar went into the hovel, the sin went out. Father broke down and admitted the evil of his ways, all the family were saved,

Preceding page: *The most popular magic lantern story of all time: 'Christmas in Paradise', a slide set produced by Bamforths in 1885, based on the ballad 'Christmas Day in the Workhouse' written by crusading journalist George Sims in 1881. 'It is Christmas Day in the workhouse / And the cold bare walls are bright / With garlands of green and holly / And the place is a pleasant sight / For the clean-washed hands and faces / In a long and hungry line / The paupers sit at the tables / For this is the hour they dine. . .'*

A scene from 'The Gin Fiend', a temperance melodrama of the 1890s in which a woman is brutally murdered by her drunken husband. Tortured by the memory of his evil deed, he ends his days in a lunatic asylum

A scene from 'Self-Made Fetters', a moral tale produced by Bamforths in the 1890s, based on a poem by Rev. M. B. Moorhouse. It tells the story of a drunkard so inebriated he can't even walk: '"Help!" he cried, "policeman!" / "Save me from this hobble / Even if your duty makes you run me in" / But the blue-coat passing laughs / at all his trouble / Counting him well punished for his foolish sin'

Scene from 'The Gates of The West', based on a poem by Adelaide Proctor. The poem inspired Arthur Sullivan to write 'The Lost Chord' which was frequently sung during the showing of this religious slide sequence: 'Seated one day at the organ / I was very ill at ease . . .'

father got a job immediately and they all lived happy ever after. This was the bit I found hard to swallow. I knew that even good men, when they lost their job, didn't easily get another. Then the lights went out and we sang another hymn and made for the door, taking a ticket and signing the pledge, week after week. 'I promise to abstain from all intoxicating drinks as beverages'. I didn't understand the last bit, but this one thing I knew. The ticket was my all important pass to the Lycett Christmas Party.

The Band of Hope, which boasted a membership of around 3 million children in 1900, was one of a host of temperance groups which used the magic lantern for propaganda purposes. In particular, they used what were known as 'life model' stories. These were stories told through a sequence of posed photographs using actors, each one of which would have accompanying words or music. Most of this lantern propaganda was made during the heyday of the temperance movement between the 1880s and the 1900s. Organizations like the Band of Hope saw the lantern as a powerful instrument in persuading audiences to 'take the pledge' – the pledge to renounce alcohol and remain teetotal. Constant reminders of the evils of drink through magic lantern shows were also regarded as important in maintaining the abstinence of members. There was an abundance of stories like 'The Slaves of Drink' in which there was a clear moral message – that drink led to poverty, violence and ill-treatment of children.

The largest and most captive audience for this melodramatic temperance propaganda was children. Organizations like the Band of Hope and the Church of England Temperance Society tried to turn them against alcohol before they developed a taste for beer and a habit of frequenting public houses. Until the 1900s it was still legal for children under fourteen to go into public houses, and many authorities and landlords, especially in poorer areas, were fairly relaxed about children drinking. Cathy Barnacle, born in 1900, remembers drinking in London public houses with her mother when she was only six: 'Pubs weren't strict at all about children going in. I went with me mum and aunty, and I used to have this gin spoon, which was a spoon layered with sugar then topped with gin. I'd have maybe three or four of them in an evening, I thought it was great! I had a real taste for it and I'd go rolling home with mum and aunty half drunk.'

The most popular 'life model' lantern slides of all were dramatizations of sentimental poems, ballads and stories. The great majority of these lantern melodramas derived from previously published work. Lantern shows, like television drama today, popularized books and boosted sales so much that publishers would send copies of every book suitable for illustration to lantern slide makers. Many classics like Dickens or Shakespeare would be boiled down to a sequence of perhaps 12 or 24 slides. More commonly the slide makers adapted stories and ballads from minor popular writers. These were usually very respectable and religious middle-class ladies writing moralistic and sentimental stories for recital to working-class audiences. They provided perfect fodder for the lantern manufacturers who were appealing to a similar audience, many of whom were semi-literate.

Mary Sewell – mother of Anna Sewell of *Black Beauty* fame – was one author whose work adapted very successfully to the lantern. Her ballad 'Mother's Last Words', a best seller in the 1860s, was turned into an immensely popular slide sequence. It told the story of 'two little boys in threadbare clothes', left destitute by the death of their mother, and their struggle to

'The Malle Scub', often known as 'Lost in The Bush', a Bamforths' life model slide set, c. *1890. It was based on the true story of three children from Melbourne, Australia, who got lost in the Bush and during their eight-day ordeal ate nothing and only drank once. They were rescued by their father. Their survival was seen as evidence of God's guiding hand*

DRINK

CRIME.
ACCIDENT.
UNTIDINESS.
SICKNESS.
EVIL.
SORROW.

A bleak warning about the dangers of alcohol which would have been part of many a magic lantern show. The Victorians had a great love of wordplay and visual puns

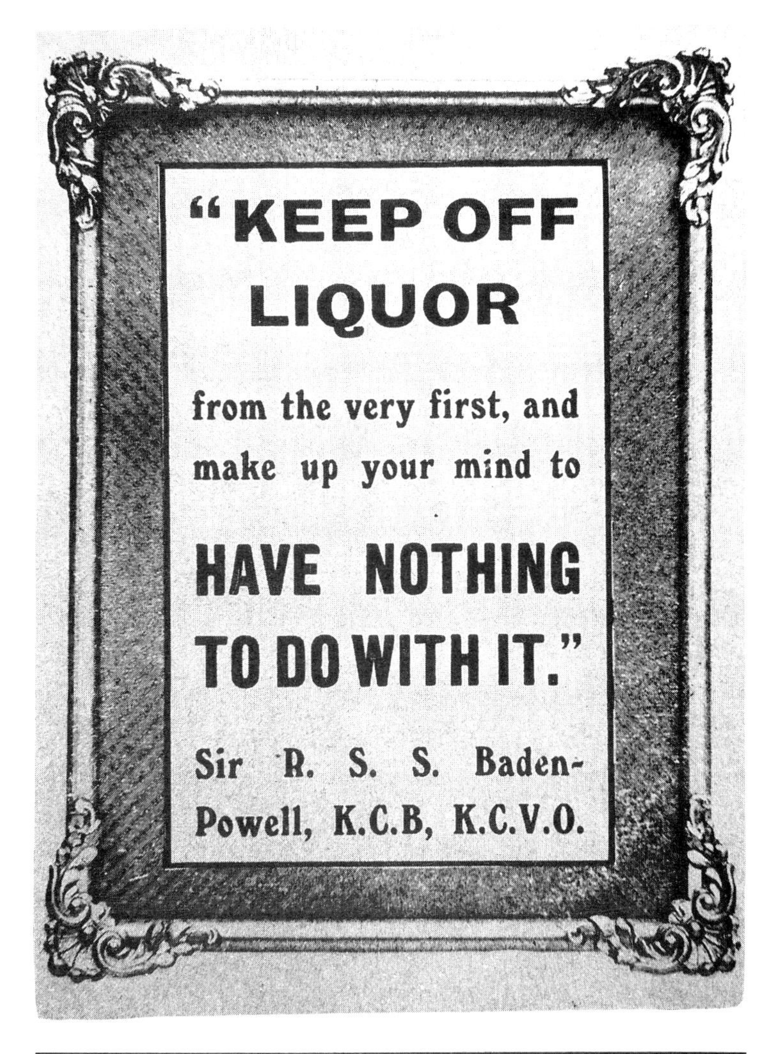

A warning against the evils of alcohol, from a series of 'Speaking Pictures' produced by the Band of Hope Union in the 1900s. The use of the name of Baden-Powell, the hero of the Relief of Mafeking in 1900 and founder of the Boy Scouts, was designed to stir up enthusiasm for temperance among the young. He was the schoolboy idol of his age and heavily involved in many of the late Victorian and Edwardian movements to foster 'social purity' and patriotism among the younger generation

Many Band of Hope and temperance lantern shows ended with this stark plea. Those in attendance – many of them children – would every week pledge to renounce alcohol and remain teetotal

resist evil in their life on the streets. Their reward is a family reunion in heaven. A host of other titles like 'Poverty's Pupil', 'Dick's Fairy' and 'Nobody Loves Me' portrayed life as a battle of good against evil, and constantly re-worked the themes of ruin and redemption. A booklet would be provided with each of these slide sets, from which the story was read aloud. Often there would be a song or hymn flashed up on the screen – sometimes at the emotional climax – so that the audience could join in, accompanied by a piano or harmonium.

Far and away the most popular 'life model' stories emanated from the pen of journalist and writer George Sims. His ballads, which at first were professionally recited, were a gold mine for lantern slide makers. Striking sets were made illustrating ballads like 'In The Signal Box', 'The Lifeboat' and 'Nellie's Prayer'. Some of Sims's ballads had a radical political message. He was deeply concerned with the suffering of the poor and he often highlighted social injustice in his stories, conveying his belief that the working classes were morally superior to the rich. One of his most radical ballads, 'In the Workhouse, Christmas Day', written in 1881, became the most popular 'life model' magic lantern story of all time.

'The Lantern', published by the Band of Hope Union in the 1880s. Biblical quotations were the inspiration for many slide shows produced by moral and religious groups at this time

Some of the 'life model' sequences achieved a powerful surrealistic effect, far ahead of their time. This was done by using fantasy and flashback techniques normally associated with the twentieth-century cinema. In 'What Are The Wild Waves Saying?' a bedroom wall dissolves into a stormy sea, threatening to engulf the children asleep in the room. In 'Rocked in the Cradle of the Deep' a sailor boy lies stretched out beside an anchor on the ocean floor, surrounded by angels. Most contemporaries agreed, however, that the greatest impact was achieved in 'Jane Conquest'. This is the story of a young mother living in a fisherman's cottage by the sea who is forced, one stormy night, to choose between tending her dying child and leaving him to alert the lifeboat that a ship – on board which is her husband – is ablaze and sinking. The interwoven themes of death, fire, faith and shipwreck allowed the performing lanternist to use every kind of special effect. Apparitions of angels, weird chords on the harmonium and blood-curdling screams made this the most gripping and popular of the surrealistic lantern sequences.

To produce these 'life model' sequences required something like an early film studio with actors, costume, props and

The first verse of the temperance hymn 'Rescue The Perishing', c. 1880. This kind of hymn would have been sung by both adults and children in the mission halls and chapels of late Victorian Britain. The slides used stereotyped characters (note the slouch and the hands in pockets of the drunkard), which never left the audience in any doubt about 'right' and 'wrong' behaviour

Scene from 'In the Signal Box', a set of six hand-tinted photographs, based on the poem by George Sims, c. *1890. This typically melodramatic story tells of a signalman whose child strays onto the railway line. He is faced with the agonising choice of switching the points as the mail train approaches – and hence causing a crash with a stationary passenger train – or of seeing his child killed. The public-spirited signalman decides in an instant that he cannot risk the lives of innocent passengers. But his wife, who unbeknown to him is in the stationary train, saves the day. 'She leapt on the line and saved him just as the mail dashed through'*

Scene from 'A Bunch of Cherries', c. *1880, based on a poem by George Sims. The story follows a posy of primroses from the moment they are picked, to their sale (see flower seller, left of picture), and finally to their purchase by a mother for her young dying daughter, who gazes upon them as she breathes her last*

Scene from 'Alone on a Raft', a set of six hand-tinted photographs produced by Bamforths in 1892. This melodrama tells of the rescue of a little boy. 'He gazed with a look oh so eager / O'er the waves of the silent deep'

A poignant moment from 'The Gin Fiend', showing the brutally beaten wife contemplating suicide to escape her drunk of a husband. This melodrama was typical of the moral tales used by temperance groups like the Band of Hope to impress upon children the potential perils of drink. Until the 1890s it was legal for children under fourteen to go into public houses, so great efforts were made to drive the message home at an early age

scenery. By the 1890s there were more than a dozen such studios dotted around Britain, the largest of which was run by the Bamforth family in the small West Yorkshire town of Holmfirth. Exploiting new developments in photography, James Bamforth pioneered the use of life models for lantern slides in the late 1870s. Until then engravings had been used to illustrate most lantern stories. Bamforth was a remarkable man who combined artistic flair with entrepreneurial drive. In the life model studios he worked as scene painter, stage carpenter, glazier, photographer and in a host of other jobs, as well as posing in a variety of roles from bishop to 'drunken loafer'. His backgrounds were usually painted, though he often also used props like a rug, a plush sofa or a rickety bedstead – many of which can be spotted appearing in story after story. However humble the sets he constructed, they all have a strong Victorian atmosphere and are steeped in period interest. The studio work was concentrated between April and September, taking advantage of the best light and weather conditions, while the winter months were devoted to manufacture, planning and design. In 1899 the magazine *The Photogram* carried a detailed description of Bamforth's operations in Holmfirth, a time when their magic lantern empire was at its height.

> The premises in which the business is conducted are curious in the extreme, consisting as they do of a series of successive studios and workshops perched at various points on a precipitous slope between the house, which overlooks the valley and the village of Holmfirth, and the first studio which is well down towards the valley. This slope, almost impossible of cultivation as a field, has been banked, terraced, and dotted with flights of steps, fountains, shady walks, leafy dells and pleasant summer houses, in a variety that might be thought impossible in such a space. Thus, within a few yards of the studios can be found almost infinite changes of setting for 'life models' in rural life. And yet, convenient as are these surroundings, it is surprising to us, after looking through many hundreds of these slides, to see how comparatively little these 'real' accessories are used. The fact is, that the controllable lighting of the studio is so very convenient for the figures, that Mr Bamforth finds his use of open-air surroundings steadily decreasing.
>
> The life-model studio is a room of 31 ft by 18 ft with a

The second verse of the hymn 'Sow in The Morn Thy Seed', published by the prolific lantern slide manufacturers Graystone Bird of Bath in the 1890s. Illustrated hymns enjoyed a brief fashionability around this time and were commonly used in churches and chapels

The good, the fruitful ground,
Expect not here nor there,
O'er hill and dale, by plots 'tis found;
Go forth then everywhere.

'The Railway Train', a Church Army slide of the 1890s. Evangelical groups often used 'modern' melodramatic images to convey their message of retribution and salvation to lantern audiences

> scene-dock and a property-room at each end; and with roof-light at both sides. Two new rooms of the same size are to be built this year, but even when they are completed, it is probable that the properties will soon be – as they are at present – overflowing all over the place. The need for almost every utensil, apparatus, and tool of almost every trade and calling, and the absolute necessity of frequent variety of furniture, costume, carpet, wallpaper, pictures, crockery etc. makes the collection of sixteen years a most fearful and wonderful affair. In one of the slide rooms are two or three 'grandfather' clocks waiting to be sold and replaced, because they have appeared so often; and everywhere in the studios and work-rooms, in the garden, in special sheds and houses, the 'props' are in evidence.
>
> The backgrounds are sometimes painted flats, but more often they consist of flats combined with a good deal of built-up structure. The flats are 14 ft by 10 ft (both sides used) and are painted by Mr Bamforth from all sorts of originals – photograms, sketches, book-illustrations – as well as from original designs. Generally they are painted out after being used for a few subjects only, and sometimes after serving as the original for only one slide. Of backgrounds that can be used in various stories, however, a stock of at least a hundred is kept.
>
> Although most of the work is done in the studio or in the terraced garden there are some scenes which can be more satisfactorily arranged in the open, as for instance, the railway station scenes on the departure or the return of a soldier son or a sailor lover. Fortunately, the railway officials are always willing (subject to the calls of duty) to place a train in any position and to give all possible facilities for the weeping or the rejoicing crowd.

The cast for Bamforth's lantern stories were all amateurs drawn from in and around Holmfirth itself. (Most lantern slide makers used 'real people' from the towns or villages where they were based.) In Holmfirth apprentices, schoolteachers, labourers, domestics, policemen and even the village blacksmith were all recruited to appear, sometimes in their real life roles. Bamforth's own staff were also often called upon to make appearances. Most did it for fun and there was rarely any special payment. Bamforth would even recruit from the local pubs as *The Photogram* of 1899 recorded:

> A public house interior is, perhaps, the easiest possible scene to fill with realistic sitters, for though Holmfirth is a busy little town there are always some idlers in the nearest 'pub', and they know that whatever else in the studio may be a fraud the beer is real. These good folk see no possible objection to posing as a room-full of 'awful examples' for a temperance reading and curiously enough, there are some, harmless enough in real life, who make beautiful models as 'leading drunkards', wife beaters etc. and who are quite willing to oblige by doing so.

Some of these actors seem to have only made one appearance. Two famous lantern slide characters, Annie and Joe, in 'Ostler Joe', are never seen again. Others were used time after time. Yet despite the fact that they were amateurs, most put on impressive performances and it is rare to spot an actor whose expression or gesture does not fit the sentimental and melodramatic mood of the stories. Bamforth revealed the secrets of his stage direction in an interview in *The Harmsworth Magazine* for 1900:

> The models are only ordinary people but I can generally get them to pose properly and to wear suitable expressions by not giving them much time to think about the matter themselves. I generally pose them very quickly if much action is to be shown. For instance in the picture called 'The Man Hunt' I took the part of the baker myself. The man who represented the thief was a very poor actor, but I gave him a sudden shake and had the photograph taken before he had time to alter his position. Very often I have to excite the models by shouting, or in other ways startling them into the position I require. With children it is quite different – I can usually train them to do whatever I want.

Children were ever-present characters in most magic lantern melodramas, heightening the pathos and sentiment for the story lines. Here again Bamforth seems to have had no recruitment problems. If large numbers of children were needed – for example, in a street scene or a tea party – he would speak to the local schoolmaster and fifty or sixty eager children would arrive at his gates after school hours. And child 'stars' would be 'discovered' and 'hired' as the Bamforth family went about their daily business in Holmfirth. Annie Cooling remem-

A slide from 'Little Jim', a moral tale produced by Bamforths in the 1890s, based on a poem by George Sims. The story revolves around a death bed scene, in which a mother, who had always bitterly complained about her 'difficult' son, now realizes how much she loves him as he dies before her eyes: 'No clatt'ring shoes / go running through / the silent room / now wrapped in gloom'

bers how she was discovered around the turn of the century by James Bamforth's son Frank: 'Frank used to come to father's shop to be shaved and would say they were photographing on Saturday morning and could the children come up.' The children were often given a few pennies for their trouble, but never more than 4d (just over 1½p). However, there was always the chance of some extra food, for example when the children were playing street urchins with crusts of bread. 'Frank kept saying "nibble the bread, make it look more realistic". And by the time they had taken the photograph we had eaten the lot and they had to send up for some more.' Annie remembers that most of all the children did it 'for fun'.

By the turn of the century 'life model' melodramas had become one of the most popular art forms and entertainments in Britain. They were the 'soaps' of the Victorian era and their position seemed as unassailable as 'EastEnders' and 'Coronation Street' do today. In 1900 Bamforth's magic lantern factory claimed to be 'The Largest Producer of Life Model Slides In The World', turning out six hundred new slide subjects every year. Bamforth's formula for success was the mass production of morality and sentiment through simple picture stories. It was a 'posed product' that was perfectly in tune with the mood of the Victorian age.

Overleaf: *'Jane Conquest' was one of the most popular lantern melodramas of late Victorian times, noted for the many surreal special effects – like apparitions of angels – used to heighten the impact of the story. It was based on a poem by James Milne, originally published in* The Methodist Family, *which was used as the reading to accompany the pictures. An abridged version appears overleaf. It is the story of a young mother who is forced one stormy night to choose between tending her dying child and leaving him to alert the lifeboat that a ship – with her husband aboard – is ablaze and sinking*

'The Little Hero', c. 1890, a moral tale about a boy whose wicked stepfather secretly puts him on board a ship to get rid of him. When the young stowaway is discovered by the angry crew they refuse to believe his story and threaten to kill him unless he tells the truth. Seconds before he is about to die they decide his story must be true as he does not waver from it. 'What I have told you is no lie / The little boy did say / If you'd let me 'ere I die / I'd like to kneel and pray . . .'

A scene from 'The Magic Wand', a lantern melodrama of the 1880s, based on a ballad by George Sims. It tells the story of Sally, a waif from the London slums. She plays the part of a fairy in a pantomime and steals the magic wand, then runs home with it, hoping its 'magic' will cure her mother's fatal illness. She is secretly followed by the School Board man who witnesses the death bed scene: 'He told how he watched her waving / The wand by her mother's bed / O'er a face where the faint grey shadows / Of the last long sleep had spread'

*'Twas about the time of Christmas, and
many years ago,
When the sky was black with wrath and
rack, and the earth was white with
snow . . .*

*Hemmed in by hungry billows, whose
madness foamed at lip,
Half a mile from the shore, or hardly
more, she saw a gallant ship*

*Still thro' the tempest bravely Jane
Conquest fought her way,
By snowy deep and slippery steep to
where the old church lay.*

*So she crept through a narrow window
and climbed the belfry stair,
And grasped the rope, sole cord of hope,
for the mariners in despair.*

And the lifeboat midst the breakers with a brave and gallant few,
O'ercame each check and reached the wreck and saved the hapless crew!

But the ringer in the belfry lay motionless and cold,
With the cord of hope, the church bell-rope, still in her frozen hold.

Poor Harry Conquest seeks his home and gains his cottage door,
But ah! no light nor faces bright to welcome him once more!

The suff'ring boy – her darling boy – whom Jane had left so ill,
Is found within his little cot . . . the wasting sickness stay'd.

CHAPTER FOUR

FARAWAY PLACES

Ted Harrison still remembers the first travel slides he ever saw as a child, in a mission hall in the East End of London around the turn of the century.

> We saw the pyramids, Egypt, seaside resorts, cathedrals in faraway towns, it was like the bleedin' seven wonders of the world. Because in those days you lived your life in the area where you were brought up and didn't go anywhere. To cross the River Lea was like going abroad. The only places I ever went to outside of Hoxton was Epping Forest for a treat and the hopfields in Kent when we went hop picking. So when we saw these different places on the old lantern our eyes nearly popped out of our heads, it was wonderful.

A magic lantern show was not considered complete unless it included a travelogue. Views of faraway places were often a source of wonder to Victorian and Edwardian audiences. After the upheaval of the Industrial Revolution and the mass movement from the country into the towns, most working people settled in their home communities and travelled very little. Most only had a few days' holiday each year: holidays with pay were a privilege restricted to better-off office workers, and travel on the new railways was an expensive luxury for the working classes. Consequently it was only through the magic lantern travelogue that many working people and their children ever got to see a variety of places beyond their home town or village. Until the mid-nineteenth century these views would be hand-painted, but the coming of photography led to the mass production of photographic 'travel' images.

One of the most photographed places of all was London. The great monuments to its power and history like the Houses of Parliament, Westminster Abbey and the Tower of London were as popular in magic lantern shows as they are in picture postcards today. Similarly in lantern slide series like 'Great Towns and Cities', the focus was on abbeys, cathedrals, town halls and a host of other public buildings. 'People' were rarely seen as important in these photographs and were often deliberately excluded. Nevertheless these views do occasionally reveal fascinating glimpses of everyday life in Victorian Britain. We see, for example, bootless urchins in the foreground of a shot of civic buildings, and traffic jams of horse-drawn trams packed with commuters in the Strand, while the early

Preceding page: *Many travelogues were presented as journeys. This unidentified train,* c. *1880, was used to set the scene in a travelogue on holiday resorts on the South East coast. By late Victorian times the train was the most popular form of transport*

Fountains Abbey in the Vale of York, c. *1875. Founded by Benedictine Monks from York in the twelfth century, this crumbling edifice was a popular place of pilgrimage for Victorian 'tourists'*

Choristers at St George's Cathedral, Windsor, c. *1865*

A 'picture postcard' view, which has changed little over the years, of the ruins of Corfe Castle in Dorset towering above the old village of Corfe, c. *1895*

The Lynton Coach begins its journey from Ilfracombe in 1880. In early lantern travelogue sequences, a picture of a horse-drawn coach would often be used to change the scene from one town or village to another but, by the end of the century, passenger trains were used more or less exclusively to serve this purpose – reflecting the major shift from horse-drawn to railway travel during the course of the century

morning atmosphere of the London markets is graphically conveyed.

Picturesque landscapes and rural scenes also became increasingly popular amongst lantern audiences in the nineteenth century. This was in part a reflection of the romanticism of the Victorian age and its rediscovery of the beauty of nature and the countryside. The Victorians nostalgically looked back to pre-industrial Britain as a kind of paradise lost, unspoilt by factories, industrial towns and railways. Country rambles, fell walking and mountaineering all became fashionable activities and more daring middle-class families began taking holidays in Snowdonia, the Lake District or the Scottish Highlands. Their romantic view of the countryside was mirrored in a glut of lantern views of streams, waterfalls, mountains, thatched cottages, quaint villages and ruined castles. Slide sequences would usually focus on particular areas with titles like 'Rambles in Yorkshire', 'Devon and Cornwall' and 'A Tour of Ireland'. And as places like Stonehenge, Ben Nevis and Land's End established themselves as tourist attractions for those seeking mystery and rugged beauty, so they became regular features in lantern travelogues. These travelogues were most interesting when they made some attempt to document the fast disappearing way of life of people who lived in particularly remote rural areas. Some of the most haunting images are of women at work – spinning, weaving, peat digging, washing and fishing – in Ireland and the Scottish Isles.

Most of the photographs were very stylized and strongly reminiscent of the romantic paintings of the period. Photographers would set up their tripods where the watercolourists had placed their easels, for example by the river Usk overlooking Tintern Abbey, and they would reproduce scenes of rural tranquillity. Many came to see photography as superior to drawing or painting, so the magic lantern for a time cornered a market once dominated by artists. Some of the most outstanding photographs in this genre were taken by George Washington Wilson, Photographer Royal for Scotland, between the 1860s and the 1880s. He printed his photographic images onto square glass plates, hired staff to hand-colour his pictures and sold the end product to many magic lantern slide companies eager for this kind of material. His photographic journey around the Hebrides, 'The Road to The Isles', was a best seller of its day.

Seaside holiday resorts were another favourite subject for

Victorian tourists alight from a paddle steamer to view Lambeth Palace in London. Taken from the lantern set 'Modern Babylon', photographed by George Washington Wilson in the 1880s

The Houses of Parliament in the 1880s, a time when the banks of the Thames were studded with wharfs and warehouses right up into the heart of London, and thousands of lightermen ferried cargoes along the river

Costermongers at work at Covent Garden, London, then the foremost market for fruit and vegetables, in the 1890s. Costermongers formed part of a growing army of labour whose livelihood depended on the consumer demand generated by the growing metropolis

Top-hatted city gents enjoy a lunchtime stroll in Ludgate, central London, in the 1890s. In the course of the nineteenth century the City and its surrounding area had been transformed into the business heart of London, housing a mass of counting houses, insurance companies and money markets

A view towards the Strand in London on a sunny day in the 1890s. The lady (left of picture) *holds a parasol to keep the sun at bay. At this time a fair complexion was fashionable; tanned skin was thought to be 'common' because it was closely associated with labourers and navvies who toiled in the open air all day*

A snarl up in the Strand, London, with a policeman directing traffic, c. *1890. With the underground in its infancy and railways unable to reach the inner areas, the horse-drawn omnibus and cab remained the most important means of getting in and out of central London throughout the Victorian era*

A street trader loaded up for a day's work near Smithfield Market, London, c. *1890. Traders would often push their barrows many miles searching for customers, sometimes gravitating to fashionable suburbs like Belgravia and Paddington. Their street cries, which began at seven in the morning and continued throughout the day, provoked petitions from angry ratepayers who wanted to ban them for disturbing the peace*

A water cart clears the dust and dirt from the streets of central London, c. *1890. Although we are accustomed to think of the horse-drawn era in a rather romantic way, it created its own pollution problems. An army of crossing sweepers (see, for example, the boy, centre picture) were employed, clearing the roads of horse dung and rubbish, which in wet weather could quickly turn into a soggy mess that was treacherous to cross*

the magic lantern travelogue. From early Victorian times the seaside holiday became established as an annual ritual of family life. Its popularity was encouraged by the creation of a national railway network linking the new towns and cities with the coast, and the development of cheap excursion trains, first pioneered by Thomas Cook in the 1840s. Middle-class families holidaying in Britain would often go away for a week or two to 'refined', exclusive resorts like Torquay in South Devon or Ventnor on the Isle of Wight. For the working classes it would more often be a cheap day excursion or a few days in a cheap boarding house in a popular resort like Southend, Margate or Blackpool. Poorer people often returned to the same resort year after year. For them seaside slides offered a momentary escape from their workaday world in the towns and cities, providing tantalizing glimpses of resorts that they would never expect to see in real life. For the better-off, however, the seaside slides probably acted as a kind of early holiday brochure, and many families must have decided to book a holiday in Sandown or Scarborough after seeing enticing views in a magic lantern show.

Some of the most exciting travelogues for Victorian audiences were those which showed scenes from other countries and cultures. Egypt, the land of the Pharaohs, was a particular favourite. Francis Frith, one of the leading Victorian photographers, took over 100,000 pictures of the Middle East, a number of which were shown as lantern slides. Skiing and mountaineering in the Alps also became popular images, reflecting their growing importance as pastimes amongst the well-to-do when on holiday abroad. Many travel sequences were presented as journeys beginning with a slide of a train leaving London's Victoria station. Then the tour would continue to the Rhineland, the United States, Greece, or wherever, taking in views of all the main tourist attractions there and back. Some lantern adventures like 'Round the World in a Hundred Minutes', produced by Riley's of Bradford, were more ambitious, offering a comprehensive global journey.

By late Victorian times the fashion for photography and the mass production of cameras meant that more and more middle-class men and women were beginning to take their own holiday 'snapshots'. Scenic views, historical monuments and family members posing on beaches or in front of exotic buildings were the greatest favourites amongst this new breed of amateur photographer. Many of their photographs were turned into

A roller coaster plunges into the water on the south coast around the turn of the century. This was then a novel seaside entertainment recently imported from the United States

The extraordinary 'giant wheel' of Earl's Court, London, inaugurated on 11 July 1895. It was powered by two huge steam engines, and the forty carriages, each of which was twenty-five feet long, could carry 1,600 passengers. One revolution could produce £120 at the box office (then a huge sum) if the wheel was full

A stark contrast between the civic splendour of Glasgow's municipal buildings and the bootless urchins in the foreground, c. *1890. People were often deliberately excluded from travelogue pictures of 'great' towns and cities, but when they do appear they provide fascinating glimpses into everyday Victorian life*

Views of cathedrals like this one – St Giles's, Bath – were always popular with lanternists. Travelogues focused on Britain's heritage and whisked audiences away to great cities and new places, rather like travel programmes on television today

The fish market at Galway, Ireland, c. 1895. Although we are accustomed to thinking of fishing as a man's trade exclusively, the industry was dependent on the labour of vast numbers of women, mending drift nets, gutting, kippering and selling fresh fish locally

A crofter's wife spinning, by George Washington Wilson, c. 1885. One of his many sentimental portraits of traditional life and the subsistence economy in the Highlands and Islands

lantern slides to entertain and impress family and friends on dark winter evenings. The well-to-do would sometimes put on magic lantern shows for their staff, illustrating their latest trip abroad. The holiday snapshot was to grow in importance in the twentieth century as, with growing affluence, the custom spread to all classes of society. With the coming of colour transparencies and slide projectors the family picture show, featuring last year's holiday snaps, was a tradition which long outlived the magic lantern.

Mountaineering was a very popular Victorian pastime. In fact, it was the British who first introduced climbing to the Swiss: even ladies in long skirts were seen to scale the peaks of the Matterhorn, for example. These photographs were taken by Abraham of Keswick in the Lake District, c. *1890*

Women collecting shellfish at Morecambe Bay, c. 1890. Many locals spent what free time they had gathering periwinkles from the shore as a way of supplementing their diet. The presence of the donkeys suggests that these women were in business, making a living from selling shellfish

Dawlish, South Devon, pictured in the 1870s when it was rapidly changing from a quaint village into a fashionable seaside resort. The key factor in its development was the coming of the railway which linked the south coast of Devon to Bristol and London

A Spitzbergen whaling boat pictured in the 1890s. The late Victorian period saw the slaughter of whole populations of whales with new cannon-fired harpoons. Whaling was shown as a curiosity in lantern travelogue sequences – there was no awareness of the need to preserve the species

St Ives harbour, Cornwall, pictured in the 1890s. It was a harbour of no small importance, with fishing boats, the local tin trade and passenger ferries to Ireland to keep it busy

Freshwater Bay on the Isle of Wight in 1890. Along with other tiny hamlets on the island, it grew rapidly in the nineteenth century into a resort which boasted a population of over 3,000 when this photograph was taken. It particularly benefited from the Victorian fashion for marine biology, being especially noted for its interesting geology and rock pools

Fishermen spread out the harvest of the sea on the beach at St Ives, c. 1890. This picturesque fishing village had long been an artists' colony, and from the late nineteenth century onwards became more and more of a tourist centre as its beauty was 'discovered' by the middle classes

A Welsh woman in traditional costume, c. *1880. Slides of people wearing traditional dress were often included in travelogues to add local colour. The tall, distinctive hat, made with beaver skin, was the height of fashion for ladies in Wales during the first half of the nineteenth century. However, the hats cost around five guineas each, which made them too expensive for all except the wives and daughters of wealthy farmers. The Rev. Francis Kilvert noted that a few Welsh women were still wearing them in the 1870s, but by then the fashion had practically died out*

Stonehenge c. *1880 when it was fast becoming a tourist attraction among the middle classes. It was around this time that the conservation and preservation of the site began to be taken seriously. In the early Victorian period visitors had done considerable damage to the stones by carving out pieces as keepsakes; the blacksmith at nearby Amesbury used to hire out hammers to help people hack at them. Before this, local farmers had broken up some of the stones to repair roads and build farm tracks*

A panoramic view across Edinburgh in the 1880s taken from St Anthony's Chapel. The lantern photographer was George Washington Wilson. Edinburgh appears more often in lantern sets than anywhere else in Scotland, reflecting its early development as a tourist attraction

The Esplanade at Ventnor, Isle of Wight, c. 1890. Resorts like Ventnor and Shanklin developed rapidly in late Victorian times, benefiting from the fashionability bestowed on the island by Queen Victoria's residence, Osborne House, and the new Express Steam Packet Services which linked the Isle of Wight with mainland ports like Southampton and Portsmouth. Ventnor became especially popular as a Victorian retirement centre and as a winter residence for 'the delicate invalid'

CHAPTER FIVE

REAL LIFE

In 1899 *The Optical Magic Lantern Journal* published an account by an anonymous lanternist and photographer of his first visit to the East End of London to picture slum life.

Preceding page: '*A day at the Zoo*', c. *1890. The elephant ride was usually the main treat for the children. Travelling menageries had been popular for many centuries but the public zoo which opened in 1828 in Regent's Park, London ('the Ark in the Park'), was a product of the nineteenth century*

I was nagged at the time by a church society for pictures of the outcast, and also lecturing at lantern meetings for the same society and wishing to obtain some real 'life' pictures, for the truth of which I could personally vouch, I consulted a friend of mine as to the way to go to work. He, having been 'through the mill' himself, kindly offered to come with me and pilot me through the district, which offer I gladly accepted.

We started from the City early in the afternoon armed with an 'Artist' hand camera with dark slides and made our way towards the haunts of the 'great unwashed' situated in or about Commercial Road East and Whitechapel. In most cases it was almost impossible to get a really good view of any of the subjects that I wished to obtain owing to the sharp look out that these men keep against observation. We were mistaken later on for police officers obtaining portraits of suspected persons.

Spotting two 'out o' works' along the road, we crossed over to the opposite side to them, passed hurriedly ahead, recrossed and stopped in a doorway under the pretence of photographing some building works going on opposite, towards which my companion pointed as the men came into view. We succeeded by this means in obtaining a fair view of these two men on whose faces despair, starvation and sadness seemed stamped indelibly and who were marching along to God only knows where!

We moved forward and descrying another specimen further on we watched him for a short time, when, to our mingled surprise and disgust, we actually saw him pause, walk into the middle of the roadway, stoop down and pick up a rotten pear, which I suppose had either fallen or had been thrown from a streetmonger's barrow and begin to eat ravenously, continuously looking round to see if he was observed. I was so taken aback by this action that I forgot what an excellent picture it would have made, but recovering myself a few moments later I 'snapshotted' him whilst taking a bite at his toothsome morsel.

We passed down by the side of Regent's Canal Docks towards Medland Street, where I was surprised to see a

A dubious selling point today maybe, but a subject of fascination to the middle-class Victorians. The frontispiece of a set of fifty-two lantern slides, produced by Riley Brothers of Bradford, in the 1890s. By the turn of the century 'poverty' sets were in great demand for purchase or hire and there were many to choose from in magic lantern catalogues

There was a thriving trade in caged birds – often linnets on account of their reputation for beautiful singing – on the streets of Victorian cities. These song birds were very popular among the poor – one of their few luxuries. The bird cage would often be hung outside the house, in the street or in the back yard, during the day, then brought inside as evening approached

Slum children playing jacks using small stones. Most working-class homes then were so small and overcrowded that there was no space to play indoors, so the street became the children's main play area. Victorian children created a welter of running, chasing, ball-bouncing and skipping games which were passed on by word of mouth from one generation to another: favourites included 'kiss chase', 'relievo' and British Bulldog

Prematurely aged mothers peg out their washing across the backyard. In the worst slums, women like these fought a daily battle against dirt, disease and hunger. It was a battle many lost. One out of every two of their children died before the age of five and the average life expectancy was only forty

An impoverished street trader with her own improvised 'pavement stall', then quite a common sight in the Victorian slums. Poor people, who often had no choice but to wear hand-me-downs and ill-fitting boots, would buy cheap bundles of clothes from traders like this. The lantern slide is captioned 'Thirst For Drink', indicating that it was used to illustrate the degrading effects of the 'demon drink'

A coffee stall. Coffee began essentially as a rather expensive middle-class drink but when its price came down in the nineteenth century some poorer people developed a taste for it. In the 1840s Mayhew calculated that there were around 300 street coffee stalls in London alone, many of them with a working-class clientele. The coffee sold on the cheaper stalls was often heavily adulterated, usually with ground chicory and baked carrots

> long line of men leaning against the railings of the docks amusing themselves while waiting in their own peculiar way, i.e. bending a piece of wire into fantastic shapes, counting and examining old buttons, talking and arguing. On my stopping to arrange in my finder the picture which I decided to take, I was startled by an exclamation from my companion and looking up found that some half dozen men had started across the road with the loudly expressed intimation that they weren't 'going to be took anyhow' and that if I didn't want 'a punch in the 'ed I had better clear out', this of course mixed up with a good deal of slang which was quite unintelligible to me.

This intrepid man was one of the pioneers of a new kind of documentary photograph which began to be shown at magic lantern shows from the 1880s and 90s onwards. Until then photographers had been deterred from picturing slum life by a variety of factors. Fear was one of the most important. The poorest streets could be dangerous places for outsiders, and photographers were frightened that they would be attacked and their valuable equipment stolen. Often such fears were greatly exaggerated, stemming from the middle-class perception of the poor as a seething sub-human mass. Many working-class people, especially groups of children on the streets, were happy to pose for photographers. They enjoyed the novelty of it all. But some photographers were indeed chased away from the poorest areas, particularly if they were thought to be insulting and intrusive. As late as the 1930s Humphrey Spender often met with suspicion and distrust when he was photographing the people of Bolton going about their everyday life.

Most photographers simply did not see it as their job to picture working-class life. Poverty was seen as a moral problem of laziness and drunkenness best dealt with in the staged melodramas of the 'life model' stories. It had to be wrapped up in a temperance lecture or a sentimental tale of religious conversion and salvation to be acceptable. Real-life poverty was abhorrent to most photographers. And, closer to home, suburban middle-class life was seen to be so familiar as to be boring and not worth recording. Photographers preferred to picture landscapes and architecture, appealing to genteel 'artistic' tastes. Documentary 'real life' lantern slides were extremely rare before the 1880s and the few that were taken often formed part of travelogue sequences. When people are pictured they are usually rustic or picturesque figures in rural settings. There is a vast legacy of twilights and posed leave-takings, but very little on everyday hard work or beer drinking in the fields.

This began to change, slowly, in the last two decades of the nineteenth century. A new breed of social investigators and philanthropists like Charles Booth, William Booth and Seebohm Rowntree journeyed into the nether world of the city slums to collect grim statistics about deprivation and destitution. They were part of a broader rediscovery of poverty at this time. Its extent in the heart of Britain's great cities shocked the comfortable middle classes. Their anxiety was heightened by the emergence of a socialist and trade union movement which demanded urgent social reform – some spoke of revolution. The pictures of this newly discovered poverty were mostly drawn in words, but a few photographers did follow reformers and philanthropists into the slums. For example, charities like Dr Barnardo's commissioned photographs to be taken of the children they saved from the streets. What photographs they took were often turned into magic lantern slides. However, practically all of them were portraits or posed in melodramatic 'life model' fashion. There were still few photographers – Paul Martin was one of the most outstanding – who tried to capture unposed shots of street urchins, poor families and working-class community life.

Not all the magic lantern slides on working-class street life were particularly sympathetic. One set, 'Street Life', produced by the Riley Brothers of Bradford in 1890, was designed to 'not only be interesting and educational' but also 'to evoke roars of laughter'. The pictures showed a collection of street 'characters' including 'the shoeblack', 'the Italian and his monkey' and 'the crossing sweeper'. The lantern lecture which accompanied the slides was very flippant and the 'characters' often became the butt of condescending jokes. We see a dishevelled-looking boy whose job it was to carry a red flag in front of a steam-roller to warn oncoming traffic, and are told 'he is paid next to nothing for what he does and it don't keep body and soul together'. He was so thin that 'when he had a pain he couldn't tell whether it was stomach-ache or back-ache'. Even when the Riley Brothers dealt with the most extreme poverty in their set 'Slum Life In Our Large Cities', the audience were told – in the tradition of the temperance lecture – that the distressing scenes they were about to see were caused 'very largely by drink'.

The circus comes to town, c. *1880. The Victorian years were the golden age of the circus (there were so few other competitors in the field of popular entertainment) and the most famous proprietor was 'Lord' George Sanger. In the 1880s, during their summer season in London, Sanger's circus performed to crowds of more than 35,000 each day. Incidentally, Sanger awarded himself the title 'Lord' out of pique in a legal battle with one of his arch rivals, The Buffalo Bill Wild West Show, which he lost!*

Left: *Elephants would often head a cavalcade of caged lions, acrobats, clowns and performing horses aimed at stirring up interest in the coming entertainment*

Sanger clowns, two of them wearing Mr Punch masks, c. *1880. As well as performing slapstick comedy, many Victorian clowns were also acrobats and jugglers, and many trained animals to take part in their act*

The lion tamer in 'Lord' George Sanger's circus, c. 1880. One of the Sanger lions was so tame that it would imitate the British lion, lying at the feet of Mrs Sanger, who would dress up as Britannia as part of a novelty act

Acrobats for Sanger's circus practise an elaborate balancing act, c. 1880. Most acrobatics were performed on the tight rope or the flying trapeze, but as this picture shows, tricks with ladders were also part of the Victorian acrobat's routine

A troupe of pierrots with a performing dog act attract the crowds at Hampstead Heath on Bank Holiday Monday, 1900

Pay day for the pit brow lasses at Rosebridge colliery in Wigan in the 1890s. Women were employed as surface workers for a range of menial tipping and sorting jobs on all the main coalfields. They were used as cheap labour, being paid far less than the men. They had been prohibited from working underground from the 1860s onwards

From the early 1890s there were more documentary photographs taken and they were less posed. This change was closely connected to the development of less cumbersome hand cameras which could take photographs in a fraction of a second. Prior to this photographers had to use bulky equipment and stands, and exposure times were anything from fifteen seconds to several minutes. As a result the camera could not capture movement, and people had to remain rigid while their photograph was being taken, otherwise it would blur. Now, for the first time, the 'snapshot' and naturalistic photography were possible. These developments encouraged photographers to be more ambitious. Slide sets of children at play, popular pastimes, Society events and work scenes all became more common at the turn of the century. They became especially popular amongst amateur photographers and their clubs and associations.

Some of the work sets were commissioned by companies eager to promote their image or their products. In 1895, for example, Palethorpes Ltd of Dudley, near Birmingham, offered free of charge to professional lanternists a slide sequence illustrating work in their sausage and pork pie factory. Other sets were produced by lantern manufacturers for showing in Mechanics' Institutes and worker's associations, possibly to instruct those wishing to enter a particular occupation. Other work sets seem to have had a lasting novelty value. In 1892 the Archer Catalogue, produced in Liverpool, advertised its most exciting new set: 'Photographs Taken in A Coal Pit By Artificial Light'. Amongst the slides it contained were 'cage at pit top', 'boy and horse passing through the door' and 'a collier at work'. Ten years later, Archers were still selling the same set as something new and intriguing.

Documentary photography was still very much in its infancy in late Victorian times. This in a sense adds to the value of the few 'real life' lantern slides taken at the turn of the century. Their importance is further heightened by the razor sharpness of the images that were captured. Shots that were converted into lantern slides possessed much greater clarity of detail than the photographic prints of the time. Today they help to form a unique visual record of life as it was lived in late Victorian Britain, vividly conveying the atmosphere of a lost age.

'Picking' coal from pit heads and slag heaps was commonplace in mining communities – even though it was strictly speaking illegal. Many children salvaged coal on their way to and from school to help keep the home fires burning.

Two pit brow lasses at Rosebridge Colliery, Wigan, pictured in the 1890s. The wearing of clogs was common among men and women in mines, mills and factories all over Britain – they were the cheapest and sturdiest footwear available for most working-class people

Two lantern slides show a drilling party at work, taken from a set of thirty-one images entitled 'Photographs Taken in A Coal Pit by Artificial Light,' produced by Archers of Liverpool in 1892. Photography in mines was in its infancy at this time and considered to be quite daring and exciting. Ten years later Archers were still advertising this set in their catalogue as a great novelty

'Home to the Vicarage', c. 1880. Note that the lady is riding sidesaddle, a genteel custom which retained its hold amongst many middle- and upper-class women throughout the Victorian era

Unlike garden parties at Buckingham Palace today, only courtiers and aristocrats were invited in Victorian times. This one took place in 1901, the first summer of the new reign after Queen Victoria's

Dressed ever correctly, straw boaters and all, well-to-do Victorian women enjoy a game of tennis around the turn of the century. 1884 had seen the first women arrive on the courts at Wimbledon, thus inspiring many young Victorian ladies to try their hand at this sport

Henley Regatta, pictured in July 1900. The Regatta began in 1839 and from mid-Victorian times onwards became established as one of the highlights of the London Season enjoyed by the upper classes. The welter of exclusive social events that came to make up the 'Season' began with the private view at the Royal Academy every May, followed by the Eton and Harrow cricket match, the Henley Regatta, polo at Ranelagh, lawn tennis at Wimbledon, and racing at Royal Ascot and Goodwood, ending in late July. In between were innumerable garden parties, concerts and balls where the sons and daughters of the rich met prospective marriage partners

Stokers take a break on the deck of the battleship HMS Edinburgh, c. *1890. One of the most important changes in the Navy in the nineteenth century was the introduction of the steam engine to replace sails. Ships were now powered from their engine room by battalions of stokers. The work was hard and dirty, and the conditions very hot, but the most arduous job of all was loading up with coal at the beginning of a journey*

The woodman's dinner hour, c. *1880. The end of the era of wooden ships in the 1860s and the mass production of cheap timber from the virgin forests in Northern Europe and North America meant that the numbers of woodmen rapidly shrunk in late Victorian Britain*

School children in Bath play during their lunch hour, c. 1898. Pictures of boys and girls playing together and holding hands at school are very rare as this kind of behaviour was generally thought to lead to 'immorality' and was often severely punished. Most late Victorian schools were sex segregated and mixed schools usually had separate playgrounds for boys and girls divided by high walls or railings

May Day in a Somerset village in the 1890s, one of the highlights of which was the maypole dancing by the schoolchildren. The first day in May was one of the most important dates in the country calendar for Victorian children. A May Queen would be chosen from among the older girls and she would lead a procession of children, all decked out in garlands of flowers and coloured ribbons, around the village singing May Day songs and collecting money

Buying ice creams on the beach at Great Yarmouth, c. 1890. Ice cream was then made locally, the cheaper versions from sugar, water and starch, while the more expensive varieties used real cream. The Victorian slang for ice cream was 'hokey pokey', which gave rise to the popular children's rhyme, 'hokey pokey, penny a lump, that's the stuff to make you jump'

A fascinating glimpse of Scarborough Sands in the 1890s. The forest of masts on the skyline graphically illustrates the fact that Scarborough remained a sizeable fishing port throughout the Victorian period. It had grown into a fashionable spa town for the Yorkshire gentry and sea bathing was originally introduced as an additional attraction for spa visitors. By the mid century it was fast losing its exclusivity and becoming one of the most popular resorts in Britain, as the annual custom of the seaside holiday took hold

A bathing machine is winched up a beach in South Devon in the 1890s. These machines – designed to protect bathers' bodies from prying eyes as they undressed and entered the water – were not always horse drawn as is often supposed. There was a tradition of women working in this lucrative seaside trade. Bathing machines died out in the inter-war years with the coming of more relaxed attitudes to body exposure and the rise of the cult of sunbathing – many were converted into beach huts

Holidaymakers indulge the English passion for paddling at Whitsand Bay, Cornwall, c. *1895. Cornwall's remoteness made it inaccessible to most day trippers and to mass tourism in Victorian times, but it was already fast being discovered by the middle classes. By the 1890s golf courses and tennis courts for holidaymakers were springing up in remote fishing hamlets like Gunwalloe and Mevagissey*

A small camp of Romany gypsies in the days of the picturesque horse-drawn caravan, c. *1890. Although gypsies were looked down upon and regarded with suspicion, their arrival in a Victorian village or neighbourhood rarely met with the kind of hostility that they have received since the last war*

Boys take advantage of a drinking fountain in Leadenhall, central London, c. *1895. Ornate fountains were a common sight in Victorian city streets. Many were paid for by temperance societies eager to provide a free thirst-quencher that would lure people away from the beer house and the gin palace. Many poor people used them as they did not have running tap water at home*

Hop-pickers encamped in Kent, c. *1890. The annual exodus of poor East End families to the hopfields every August and September provided them with an important extra source of income as well as a 'free' holiday out in the fresh air*

East Enders dance to the sound of the barrel organ in 1890. The street was the main arena for entertainment among poor working-class families, and dancing was especially popular with the young women and children. Often the men would be spectators, though at certain times of the year, like Christmas for example, they would ritually dress up as 'ladies' and have a 'knees up' themselves

A fancy dress carnival on roller skates in Edwardian Bristol. The fashion for roller skating originated in the United States in the last quarter of the nineteenth century and was imported into Britain in the 1890s and 1900s, with many roller skating rinks springing up in towns and cities

Somerset village children, sliding and sledging on a frozen pond, pause for their photograph to be taken, c. *1890. Despite the fact that Victorian country children often had no money and few toys, they could enjoy a host of seasonal games – skating and snowballing in the winter, bird-nesting in the spring, swimming in the summer and conkers in the autumn – all for free*

Children sailing model yachts at Eastbourne, a fairly quiet, respectable, mainly middle-class resort by 1895. In the era before paid holidays (which were only introduced after the Second World War), a holiday for a week or two by the sea was a privilege enjoyed principally by children with better off parents. Poorer families had to make do with day excursions

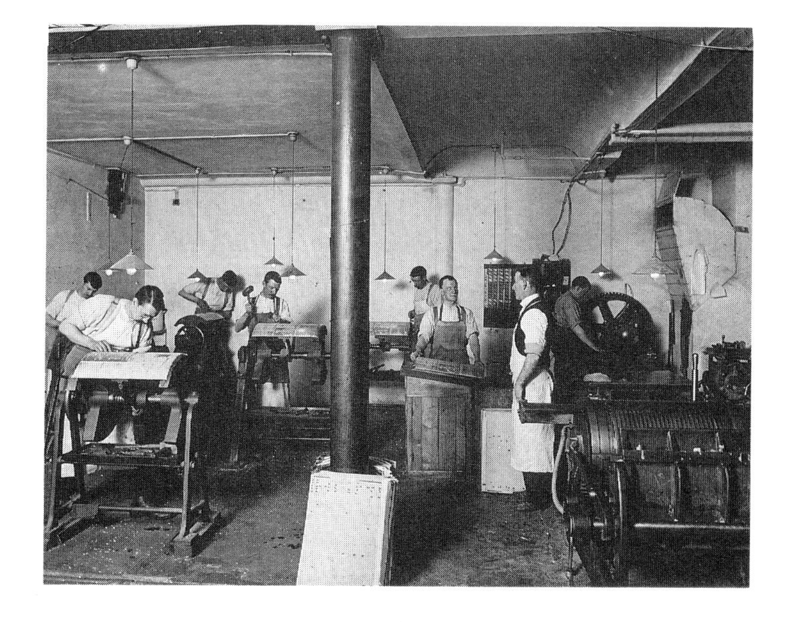

One slide from a set illustrating the production of The Daily News *in 1900, covering everything from editorial meetings to typesetting. Lantern sets on various occupations and careers were very popular in adult education classes and Mechanic's Institutes, providing a 'taster' for those thinking of starting a new career*

CHAPTER SIX

A WORLD OF COLOUR

In *The Optical Magic Lantern Journal* of 1892 H. M. Underhill described the art of hand painting on glass for magic lantern slides.

> A photograph is only a photograph after all, and will never be a picture, because it has no soul. Real painted pictures, therefore, will always be better and more interesting lantern slides than anything the camera can produce. If any 'lanternist' will look at some of the best 'hand painted' slides, for which is asked from £1 to £3 each, he will be convinced of this. To buy such slides is ruinous for all but the deepest purses, but anyone who can paint can make slides as good as these . . . It takes me from six to eighteen hours to make a finished picture. What a long time? True; but then – what a nice slide! With a little practice pictures can be painted so smoothly that no roughness is perceptible on the screen when one is seated about three or four yards distant. And as for colour – in these pictures you have real brilliancy, and the best of coloured photographs are thick and dirty by comparison. I have now painted six hundred slides or more, and I have illustrated the following subjects: Scientific lectures (two or three), Japanese art, A Tour of Norway, Hans Andersen's 'Snow Queen' and some Fairy Tales. These last are immensely popular with children of all ages from seven to seventy, and I have enthusiastic audiences.

Our images of the Victorian age are often shaped by the many black and white or sepia photographs of the period. This was an era which long pre-dated the invention of colour photography. The magic lantern, however, brought colour into the Victorian world. Most magic lantern slides were either painted on glass or were tinted photographs. There were impassioned arguments amongst lanternists as to which was the best method. Many agreed with H. M. Underhill that the hand-painted slide was often aesthetically superior to the tinted photographic slide. But it was regularly pointed out that this artistry could not be produced for the mass market amongst whom the cheap tinted photographs were immensely popular. Whatever their position on this debate, though, most agreed that both were much better than black and white photographic slides. They were seen as drab and lifeless compared to anything in colour.

A permanent attraction of the Royal Polytechnic in Regent's Street was its celebrated magic lantern shows. When in 1882 the effects of the Polytechnic were auctioned, individual slides fetched as much as 50/- each – a considerable sum of money at the time. This is a tribute to the quality of the slides which according to T. C. Hepworth had 'Delighted two generations of sightseers at the old Polytechnic . . . Some of these pictures being most elaborate works of art.' The Polytechnic used oversized projectors, so these slides would be over 15cm deep

Preceding page: *A hand-painted advertisement for Vinolia soap, c. 1895. Some companies supplied colour slides free of charge to lanternists on condition that they regularly showed them in their entertainments*

Up to the early nineteenth century all lantern slides were painted entirely by hand. Often the lanternist painted the pictures himself as there was no commercial supplier of slides at this time. Most of the pioneers of the magic lantern as an entertainment like Etienne Gaspard Robert, Paul de Philipstal and Henry Langdon Childe all painted the slides used in their shows.

Painting on glass for the magic lantern was, at its best, a highly skilled art. The slides were often only three or four inches in diameter – or even smaller – so the picture was painted in miniature, a difficult and complex process. The artists would often use a watchmaker's magnifying glass when working. They either painted directly onto the glass or made an outline drawing which they then placed under the glass as a guide. To get a rich and brilliant colour effect some artists painted first in water colour, then applied a second layer of oil paint. A small knife or needle point was used for etching fine details.

The main skill of the slide painter was not to paint for the immediate visual effect on the glass, but to create a realistic and lasting image when projected onto the screen. Obviously only transparent colours could be used. Opaque colours like

Two slides illustrating summer (right) *and autumn* (left) *from a beautiful set of dissolving views entitled 'The Four Seasons',* c. *1870, in which painted scenes of spring, summer, autumn and winter would melt into each other. In contrast to the rapid changes of images every second or two that we are accustomed to on television today, Victorian lanternists would have made the four slides last for five minutes or more, confident that the audience would find enough interesting detail to hold their attention. The poem that would have been read to accompany this slide is reproduced in the colour section*

vermilion appeared black or distorted because the light could not filter through properly. The artist was thus restricted to just a dozen or so colours. Only one shade of green, verdigris, for example, remained true when projected. Also the colours used had to be able to withstand limelight or they would fade and crack, ruining the slide. This again restricted the choice, counting out many reds. Yet despite these problems and limitations many of the early hand-painted slides were very beautiful. They were often painted in a precise, classical style, and they achieved a remarkable level of detail which stood up to very large magnification.

The most outstanding pictures in early and mid-Victorian Britain were commissioned by the Royal Polytechnic for its London exhibitions. They chose the best painters on glass and miniature artists to do the work. Painting one image sometimes took days or even weeks and was an extremely expensive business. The slides, measuring 10″ × 8″, were some of the largest ever produced. The artists, however, are for the most part anonymous. Few even initialled their work. The paintings of the few who did sign their slides like the French artist Desch, have now become highly prized collector's pieces.

The Eruption of Vesuvius, overlooking the Bay of Naples, one of a set of four hand-painted dissolving views, c. *1850. The sequence begins with an earthquake 'effect', followed by the appearance of a plume of smoke, then the dramatic eruption, and finally lava is shown as having buried the surrounding area. The story of the eruption of Vesuvius which engulfed Pompeii in AD79 had a special fascination for the Victorians. This was re-inforced by the morbid fear of a similar disaster occurring again: in the hundred years up to the 1830s Mount Vesuvius erupted eighteen times*

A blacksmith at work in the hand-coloured slide sequence 'Buy Your Own Cherries' – which in Victorian slang meant 'I'm all right Jack'. This moral tale produced in the 1890s was, like many others of its type, a celebration of the virtues of honest toil and duty to God

At the bottom end of the market most of the slides painted by the itinerant lanternists were often of poor quality, though some have a primitive charm and attraction. Few had the skill or resources to produce anything more than crude, gaudily coloured images.

But by the beginning of the Victorian period a method of printing outlines onto glasses had been developed. This meant that for the first time the commercial production of lantern slides was possible. Mass production began from the mid-century onwards when small magic lantern factories sprouted up in cities like London, Liverpool and Leeds. They farmed out the glass slides bearing the printed outlines to battalions of poor families living nearby. They were painted at home, then returned to the factory for finishing and distribution. Lantern painting was one of the many lowly paid 'sweated' industries of the Victorian era exploiting the cheap labour of women and children.

Some of the painting of lantern slides, however, was done by amateurs, for the love of it – rather like the way in which some people paint eggs, say, today. It became a very popular hobby in early Victorian times and companies like J. Barnard and Sons in Central London supplied kits containing paints, glass slides and elaborate instructions for aspiring lantern artists. Colour charts were usually included, describing how to achieve the correct colouring when the slide was projected. One guide to painting on glass recommended, for example, that the artists use Venetian red for 'distant flesh', Indian yellow for 'near flesh' and carmine for 'cows and horses near'.

From the mid-century onwards a new form of mass colour production became important, the chromo-lithographic process. The design was printed from stone onto a sheet of paper, then transferred by means of various chemicals to glass. This method was more suited to factory production from beginning to end, with no need for home workers. The most prolific producers of this kind of lantern slide were J. Theobald's of Farringdon Road, London, and in 1892 a correspondent of *The Optical Magic Lantern Journal* reported a visit there:

> Ascending still higher, we entered the next floor, which is at the top of the building. This floor is of greater interest than either of the previous ones, for here the transferring and mounting of slides was being done by a large staff. As water plays an important part in this department, many of

> the tables were provided with a gutter immediately below the edge of the sides. Going down one side of the room we observed a very interesting division of labour. The glasses, having been washed, were passed onto the next table, when they were polished with paper and racked up; these racks, as soon as full, were passed to the next table, which had large vessels containing what appeared to be gelatine.
>
> The chrome transfer backed with paper, was, after being coated from this vessel, stuck on the glasses and placed in a rack; these, as soon as dry, were passed onto the next table and immersed in water. After soaking for about five minutes, the paper backing was detached and the slide again placed in a rack to dry. At the next table, a cover glass was placed upon each picture, and the binding strip gummed on the edge. Every now and again the pile of finished slides was taken away to the sorting department, boxed, labelled, and stored along the sides of the room, to eventually be placed in the lift, which conveys them to the packing room and thence to the basement. We are informed that a consignment of 200 gross of assorted sizes of glass for slides was delivered each week throughout the year.

When this article was written in 1892, however, the most common form of lantern slide was the hand-tinted photograph. This new art had begun in the 1850s and 60s when the first photographic lantern slides were created. Factories employed armies of assistants whose sole job it was to apply colour to photographs. In some of the largest factories like Walter Tyler's in Waterloo Road, London, the painting was done by rows of workers – usually young women with good eyesight and a steady hand – standing side by side on a production line. In smaller establishments producing better quality slides like Paxton's of Holloway, there was a more artistic atmosphere and the 'ladies' were seated at easels in a 'studio'.

A surprisingly high proportion of photographic images for the lantern were hand-coloured, whether they were travelogues, news pictures, documentary portraits of street life or 'life model' melodramas. In many cases slapdash production-line methods meant that original images were spoilt. To our eyes, attuned to a world of sophisticated colour photography, they often look anaemic and artificial, but sometimes the colour does heighten the period charm and interest of the pictures.

A hand-tinted photograph of the Menai Straits Suspension Bridge, which links the Isle of Anglesey with the mainland of North Wales, taken from an 1800s travelogue sequence. The bridge, built by Thomas Telford in 1819, was one of the triumphs of nineteenth-century engineering, it being the first to use the suspension principle

The Chain Pier, Brighton, a hand-tinted photograph, c. 1875. Opened in 1823, the pier was designed on the same principle as a suspension bridge and built on four massive iron clad piles. A grand pier was seen by the Victorians as essential to a seaside town and dozens were erected in the course of the nineteenth century. The Chain Pier in Brighton was a prominent feature of the town, appearing in paintings by Turner and Constable, until it was destroyed by a storm in 1896

Hand-tinted photographic images were so popular and cheap to produce that by the 1880s they were increasingly displacing the art of painting straight onto glass. It was too slow and expensive a process to compete in the new industrial world of mass markets. Also the latest lanterns had such powerful lights that they often showed up every little imperfection in the artist's work. Tinted photographs fared much better under the spotlight. Sadly, by the end of the Victorian period the mass production of these coloured images had more or less killed off lantern slide painting as an art.

One of a series of hand-tinted colour slides illustrating Queen Victoria's Golden Jubilee celebrations in 1887. These slides were immensely popular at the time, partly because the Queen had scarcely been seen by her subjects in 'pomp or purple' or otherwise for twenty-five years. She wrote in her diary as 1887 drew to a close: 'Never can I forget this brilliant year, so full of marvellous kindness, loyalty and devotion of so many millions, which really I could hardly have expected'

Two scenes from 'The Drunkard', a classic temperance set of ten hand-tinted slides produced in the late 1870s. The story tells of a father who squanders his money on drink and ends up in the gutter. He realizes his 'wickedness', prays to God for strength and forgiveness, and in the final scene (bottom) *we see him as a reformed paterfamilias surrounded by his wife and children: 'Oh hear his call and hasten forth / To render what help you can / Remember when he struggles thus / He is a brother and a man'*

Hand-tinted photograph of one of Britain's heavily armed battleships. During the nineteenth century Britain established itself as the supreme naval power in the world

Hand-tinted photograph of sailors from the battleship HMS Edinburgh, *at the turn of the century*

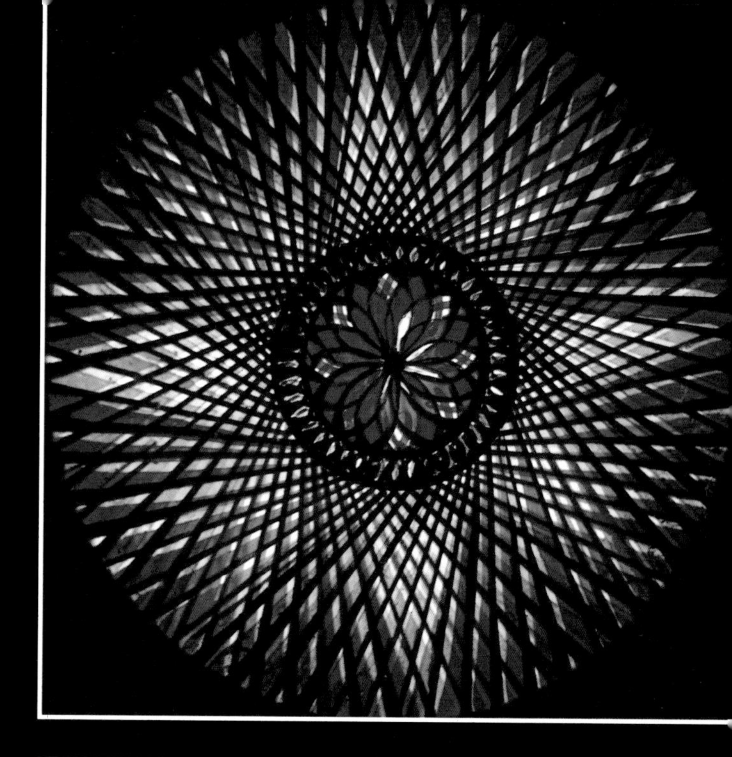

Two examples of chromatropes, sometimes called 'colour turners', c. 1860. By using two identically patterned mechanical slides like these it was possible to create a magical effect known as 'artificial fireworks.' The handle on one slide would be turned clockwise, while the handle on the other would be turned anti-clockwise. The spiralling patterns and the explosion of colour on the screen remained a great favourite with lantern audiences throughout the Victorian period.

A poem for a 'dissolving' view of the four seasons, reproduced in part on pages 112 and 113

A scene from the temperance melodrama 'The Drunkard' (see also page 119). Many of the temperance stories produced for the lantern were hand-tinted photographs – it was thought that the use of colour would heighten their impact on the audience. This slide is exceptionally well painted; many, however, were spoiled by the slapdash adding of colour.

An Isle of Man fisherman's home, c. 1890. This was one of a series of sentimental portraits of farming and fishing communities which seem to have had great appeal to middle-class Victorians, who looked back with great nostalgia to the pre-industrial days of thatched cottages and craft skills

The main street in Matlock Bath pictured in 1890 in a travelogue on the Derbyshire Dales. The Central Restaurant (centre picture) specialized in dinners for cyclists and provided parking space for their 'machines'. 'Dale' cycling was then the latest craze for the most adventurous cyclists

Left: *The tiger, a 'double slipping' mechanical slide,* c. *1860. By pulling the glass slide, the lanternist could make the tiger's face appear to come alive on the screen. His eyes would gently roll, his nose wriggled and sniffed the air, and his whiskers would twitch*

Right: *The opening slide for a lantern show,* c. *1880, introduced by Mr Punch, one of the most popular comic characters of the Victorian period. To begin with he would appear holding a blank card. Then, through a mechanical slipping slide effect, the world 'welcome' would appear on it as if by magic*

Below: *A high-quality hand-painted slipping slide, 1858. When the first glass was pulled the dog would appear to jump through the hoop. When the second glass was pulled the dog would land on the ground*

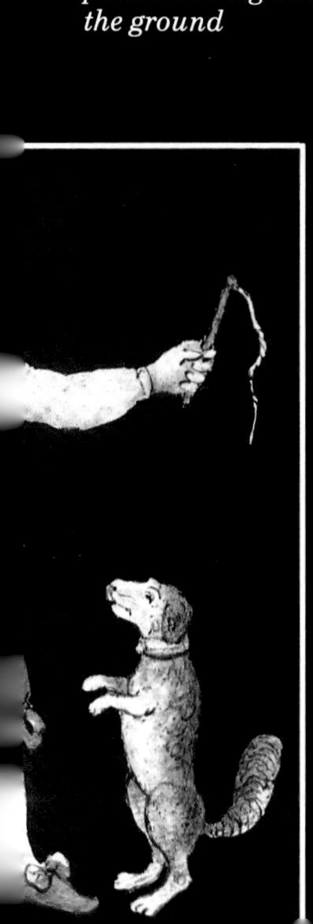

Hand-tinted photograph of a group of smartly dressed sailors, c. 1880, from one of the many sets entitled 'Life in the Navy' produced around this time. These inevitably presented a rosy and heroic view of the British sailor, mirroring the imperialism of the age

'En Route To America', from a set of sixty hand-tinted photographic slides, entitled 'An American Lecture', illustrating American towns and cities in the 1880s. This picture shows sailing ships departing from the Cove of Cork in Southern Ireland, then the point of departure for many thousands of emigrants to America. Mass emigration to the United States in the nineteenth century made American lantern lectures very popular among Victorian audiences, some of whom were considering starting a new life in the States or had relatives there

'Preparing For The Cavalry', a hand-tinted photograph, from a set of 150 slides on the British Army and Navy, c. 1885. Posed battle scenes which made war seem glamorous and heroic were the stock in trade of late Victorian lantern manufacturers

'And with his hard, huge hand, he wipes a tear out of his eyes.' A slide from 'The Village Blacksmith', a hand-painted set made in 1889 to illustrate the poem of the same name by Henry Longfellow. It is a tale of honest toil and simple religious faith, part of which focuses on the blacksmith's vision of an angel in church, a special effect created through a slipping slide.

'The Naval Engagement', taken from a set of six dissolving lantern slides, c. 1880. This battle scene would be brought to life by an array of special visual and sound effects. The French ship (on the right of the pictures) is fired on with cannon and musket shots. It explodes, leaving a burning hulk which smokes and finally sinks. These slides contain marvellous detail: note the Royal Marines standing on the spars taking musket shots at 'the enemy'. These battle scenes were enacted countless times in front of Victorian audiences. The sinking of the French ship would often be greeted with cheers!

CHAPTER SEVEN

THE HARD SELL

In 1876 *The Globe* reported that traffic in the Strand had been brought to a standstill by 'a gratuitous exhibition of dissolving views, exhibited on a large screen on the second floor of a house on the north side of the street. The subjects exhibited have been facsimiles, on an enlarged scale, of the posters which appear on street-hoardings, and give in attractive form, rapidly succeeding each other, gratuitous advice as to the best sewing machine, the cheapest hatter, where to dine and the most popular newsagent.'

This Victorian publicity stunt is one of the first recorded examples of the use of the magic lantern for advertising in Britain. In the following decades lantern advertisements were to appear in a variety of public places. In 1889 *The Optical Magic Lantern Journal* reported that most principal railway stations were showing lantern advertisements. The slides would change automatically every thirty seconds and they would be projected day and night. The clockwork mechanism which operated this slide show had to be wound up by railway staff once a week. Some of this propaganda celebrated the virtues of the railway company itself, and most companies, especially the Great Western Railway, produced slide advertisements for their most attractive routes and engines. Music halls and theatres also regularly showed lantern advertisements, though there were constant complaints from the advertisers that the displays occurred before the audience in the most expensive seats had arrived and sometimes that the 'break for advertisements' began before the doors had even been opened to the public.

Companies did not concentrate their advertising efforts solely on the commerical world of entertainment and travel. They also tried to reach their market through the humble lanternist who staged shows in village halls, church halls and temperance meetings. Bona fide lanternists would be invited to apply for slides to be supplied free of charge direct from the company. This was a great bonus for the lanternist who could add the variety and sophistication of beautifully produced advertisements to his show at no extra cost. Fry's chocolates and cocoa, Peak Frean Biscuits, Elliman's liniment and Pears' soap were amongst a host of products which were promoted in this way. The advertisements took a variety of forms: one-off slides, sets 'celebrating' how the product was made and amusing stories in which the product played a leading role. But there was a catch for unsuspecting lanternists. They would

Preceding page: *An advertisement for pickles, c. 1895. Victorian magic lantern shows were often punctuated by advertisements which used a range of surreal images, anticipating the cinema and television adverts of our day. Victorian advertisers were not slow to exploit the appeal of babies and young children to sell their products*

Advert for Fry's 'Five Boys' around the turn of the century. At this time chocolate was still very expensive and regarded by many as a luxury. Most Victorian children ate boiled sweets and toffees, not chocolates

From the 1880s right through to the 1930s the lantern was used to promote the services of rival horse-bus, motor-bus, tram, railway and trolleybus services

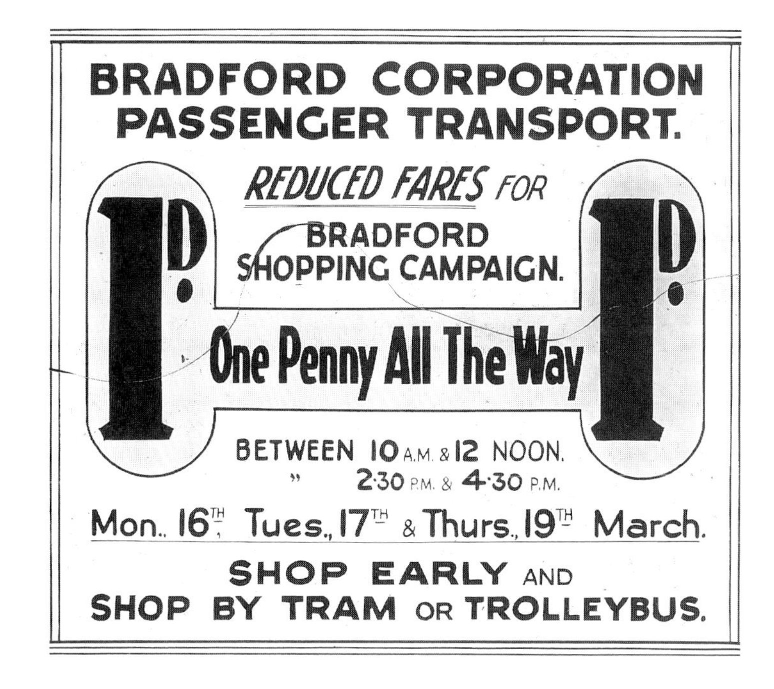

Two lantern advertisements for Bird's custard powder in the 1890s. Custard, made from eggs and milk, had been eaten for centuries, largely for medicinal purposes. Custard powder, which was based on cornflour, was invented by Alfred Bird, a Birmingham chemist, in 1837. His business prospered so much that by the 1900s Bird's custard was one of the nation's most popular family dessert dishes. The company's early advertising campaigns stressed the convenience and superiority of custard powder compared to eggs

Elliman's, like many other advertisers, eagerly exploited the cycling craze in the 1890s to promote its products. The many minor injuries caused by hundreds of thousands of Victorians pedalling furiously down bumpy roads must have considerably increased their profits. The idea of women wearing culottes would have been considered rather daring; Queen Victoria's daughter Princess Maud wore a skirt with lead weights sewn into it to prevent it billowing when she cycled

Lantern advertisements reflect the imperialism of the age. With the Empire at its height, nationalistic characters like John Bull could be counted on to help sell all sorts of goods. Patriotic packaging was especially favoured by makers of tea, biscuits, tobacco and alcohol. Often products were adorned with pictures of the royal family, famous generals and military occasions

A song slide set produced by Bamforths around the turn of the century. Opening slide (top) and chorus (bottom). The set also contains the song's several verses and a number of hand-tinted photographs of couples in romantic settings which the lanternist would show at appropriate moments when the audience was singing along. Illustrated song slides were used to advertise sheet music in late Victorian and Edwardian times and they were as essential to the success of popular songs as pop videos are today

subsequently be badgered by the company's marketing department to provide regular reports on how often the slides had been shown and details of the audience's size and composition. This early attempt at market research was a constant irritant to lanternists who sometimes wrote letters of complaint to the editor of *The Optical Magic Lantern Journal*. This correspondence illustrates how companies whose products were advertised at Band of Hope and temperance meetings often enjoyed an additional and unexpected 'plug'. Evangelical lanternists clearly felt it was their duty to cloak advertisements with the same moral message as that which was contained in their tirades against the evils of drink and self-indulgence. As Geoffrey Hudson put it in a letter to the *Journal* in 1893: 'I may say that when I exhibit advertisement slides I always try and point a moral and tell a tale. With "The Cabby and His Cocoa" (Cadbury's) I say "far better to drink cocoa than beer, he is more likely to have his head clear and his feet warm"; with "Matchless Cleanser" that "cleanliness is next to Godliness and if more soap were used there would be less dirt and so on morally". So you see it is possible to make even this class of advertisement really instructive if pains be taken.'

With the extension of the vote in late Victorian times the major political parties began to take an interest in the magic lantern as a powerful means of selling themselves to a mass electorate. The decade before the First World War was the heyday of lantern propaganda shows, forerunners of the party political television broadcast. This glorification of the party and its policies in popular picture shows began in the 1890s during the fiercely contested London County Council elections. 'The Lantern As An Electioneering Agent' was described by J. G. Bennett in *The Optical Magic Lantern Journal* of 1895.

> The Chairman, a candidate who seeks re-installing, opens with an introductory address, in which he eulogises his party in general and himself in particular, prefacing as it were the main points of the lecture that is to follow . . . The so-called lecture was the repeating of an accomplished curriculum of the Council's doings from its formation. Each and every improvement of this parliament, for the government of the largest capital in the world, was demonstrated by photography and the lantern. No point was missed by spokesman or artist, and not at all improbable is it that converts were gained from opponents. One indeed

> was bold enough to audibly exclaim 'Well I'm blowed! I've read a good deal about it, but never understood what it all meant till now.' . . . The advancement made in connection with the fire brigade was well exemplified by a series of spirited pictures and effects; this, as every lanternist knows, fairly seized on the audience. Perhaps the sets that gave most pleasure were those devoted to asylums, parks and such open spaces as come under the Council's jurisdiction. Some of the interiors of the former came as a surprise to many, the writer included. They are without doubt very beautiful institutions. Among the latter were many choice bits of picturesque scenery to be found in Waterlow, Clissold and other parks, secured by the Council for the public good for all time, and as may be imagined were each and all strong points in the candidate's favour . . .
>
> Parish councils, vestries, parliamentary constituencies, school-board contests, and a host of other bodies who have to court the vote, will not think of doing so in the very near future, without the lanternist's help, because he can show on the screen, whether it be in the public hall, school room or street, facts, figures and particulars that no other form of advertising can approach.

At around the same time as the lantern was discovered by politicians its advertising power was beginning to be recognized by the new popular music industry. Before the Great War one of the most lucrative sides of this business was sheet music sales for singalongs with the piano. In the days before mass-produced records and before radio and television promotion, the main problem that faced the music publishers was how to popularize their songs. Then in 1894 Tony Pastor, a New York theatre electrician, came up with the bright idea of producing magic lantern slides to illustrate the lyrics of a song. He was commissioned by a local music company to illustrate a new ballad, 'The Little Lost Child', using life models, and it quickly became a major hit, selling over two million copies. For the next twenty years there was a flood of illustrated song slides – most of them romantic and sentimental ballads – and they became as essential to the success of popular songs as pop videos are today. The main outlets were music halls, cinemas and the shows of amateur and professional lanternists. There would usually be two sets of slides, one with the pictures, the other with the words, and it was thought especially important

In the twentieth century the cinema hit the advertising potential of the magic lantern show by winning over audiences to the new picture palaces. However, most companies found it too expensive to make film advertisements. Instead they continued to produce lantern slides, creating a niche for the lantern in the cinema age. These two lantern advertisements were shown in Morecambe cinemas around the time of the First World War

Milk chocolate was not produced in Britain until 1897 and Fry's were among the first producers. Until then the market was dominated by high-quality Swiss manufacturers. The chocolate eating habit did not spread to all classes of society until after the First World War when mass production got underway and prices were reduced

It is surprising how many now familiar products became established in Victorian times. This Pear's Soap advertisement was particularly unusual because a mechanical lever, operated by the lanternist, caused the woman's arm to rub furiously at the little boy's face

to get audiences to join in with a song's chorus to get them to want to buy it. Their advertising power was seen to be so potent that they would sometimes be supplied free or for just a nominal charge to the best outlets.

Most of these popular illustrated song slides were made in the United States. The majority of those shown in Britain were 'imports', a reflection of the astonishing rise to ascendancy of Tin Pan Alley in the popular music industry in the years before the First World War. Even seemingly 'English' songs like 'Down At The Old Bull And Bush' were in fact penned on the other side of the Atlantic. Many illustrated song slides seen in Britain came from the New York studios of Dewitt C. Wheeler, who turned out thousands of slide sets each year. The illustrated song 'advertising' craze was a graphic example of the early Americanization of British culture which in fact began in the late Victorian years.

A surreal image from the song slide 'The Garden of Love' produced in 1906 by Scott and Van Altena of New York, one of the most prolific companies making lantern slide sequences to sell sheet music. The artwork on the American song slides which flooded into Britain around the turn of the century was often extraordinarily complex, involving the superimposition of several images to give a multi-layered effect

CHAPTER EIGHT

SAVING SOULS

FOXE'S MARTYRS.

Glasgow Protestant Missionary Society,

ESTABLISHED 1878.

LECTURE

BY

MR. GEORGE HAY,

WITH

MAGNIFICENT LIME LIGHT ILLLUSTRATIONS.

LIST OF VIEWS.

Latimer and Ridley at the Stake.
Christians Worried by Dogs.
Arrest of Polycarpus.
Perpetus resisting entreaty.
Vision of Constantine.
Waldensian Christians frozen to death.
Spanish "Auto de Fe."
Spanish Protestant women taken to execution
Death of Admiral Coligny.
A Bohemian lady drowned with her husband
Trial and degradation of John Huss.
Jerome dragged to the Cloister.
A monk cuts the throats of fourscore women.
A Waldensian lady throws herself over a precipice.
Susanna Ciacquin throws the soldier over a precipice.
Execution of Sir John Oldcastle. [Cheapside
Tonstal burning Tindal's Testament in
Martyrdom of Frith at Smithfield, 1533.
The Rack.
Bishop Ridley admonishing Princess Mary.
Execution of the Duke of Somerset, 1552.
Lady Jane Gray sees her husband taken to execution.
Dr Taylor degraded by Bonner.
Dr. Cranmer brought to trial.
Tomkin's hand burned by Bonner in a candle.
Chained Bible in a Church at New York.
William Hunter, aged 19, before his execution
Dr Cranmer regrets his recantation.
Ridley writing in prison.
Latimer preaching.
Latimer brought to Smithfield. [Cardinal.
Ridley refuses obeisance to the Pope and
Site of the Martyrdom of Bishops Cranmer, &c
Latimer and Ridley before execution.
Bonner encouraged by a shoemaker at Coventry.
Execution of Rawlins, the Fisherman.
Rev. W. Marsh reading his Bible on his way to the stake, 1555. [for striking a Priest
William Flower's hand cut off at the stake
Irish Protestants forced to the sea and drowned at Trelawny in 1664.
Martyrdom of Sieur Boelon at Montpieller by having his limbs broken with an iron bar, &c.
Scourging of George Penn in the Inquisition.
Martyrdom of John Williams in the South Sea Islands.

Amusing Incidents for Children at the Close.

In 1893 the Reverend George Allchin began work as a missionary in the Far East. For the next seven years he travelled all over Japan from Sappor in the north to Kagoshima in the south preaching with a magic lantern. He calculated that he staged 357 magic lantern shows, most of them in theatres, temples and eating houses, speaking to 157,000 people. Writing in 1900 he described the power of the lantern to attract and convert large 'heathen' audiences.

> In order to allure as many as possible and especially to draw a class who under no other circumstances would listen to a word about Christianity I entertain them for about half an hour with moving ships, dissolving views, Chromatropes and scenery. This also helps forestall any disturbance which men of the baser sort might plan for. Then when sympathy has been awakened I quietly pass on to the pictures which illustrate 'the topic of the evening'. The object being to attract and instruct the masses whose religious ideas are perverted by heredity, education and environment, the subjects of the sermons are selected with great care. The Japanese are steeped either in superstition or atheism. I could tell many touching stories of prodigal sons confessing their sins, backsliders reclaimed, decisions for Christ brought to a point after months of procrastination and awakened desires to read the Bible and to live a better life.

It is often forgotten that the army of Victorian missionaries who took Christianity to those they saw as the backward people of the world – principally the people of Africa, India, China and Japan – did not rely solely on the Bible to get their message across. From the 1860s onwards the more enterprising missionaries also took a magic lantern and as many sets of biblical slides as they could carry. The lantern with its powerful pictures and simple story lines was an ideal instrument to overcome the barriers of language and culture that confronted them. Many a lantern show was staged in a rickety mission station or mud hut in 'darkest Africa'. It was here that many tribesmen and women had their first taste of Christian imagery: the Virgin Mary, the Crucifixion and the bearded, cloaked figure of the white Victorian God. David Livingstone, the famous mid-century African explorer and missionary, described the lantern as his 'most valuable travelling friend'. He

Right: *An artist's impression of a lantern church service published in* The Harmsworth Magazine, *1900. A triunial lantern (in the organ on the left) is used to project the picture and the huge screen fills the Chancel arch. When combined with organ music, the images were described by the magazine as having a 'sensational' effect on churchgoers*

Preceding page: *A calling card used by the Glasgow Protestant Missionary Society in the 1880s (*top shows front and bottom shows back of the card*). The show being advertised is an extraordinarily gruesome catalogue of the persecution of Protestants, made up of a series of engravings. 'Foxe's Martyrs' was shown by various Protestant groups all over Britain. This kind of religious propaganda must have reinforced sectarian divisions which already ran deep in places like Glasgow. Perhaps most interesting is the note at the bottom which suggests that children would have watched these harrowing images*

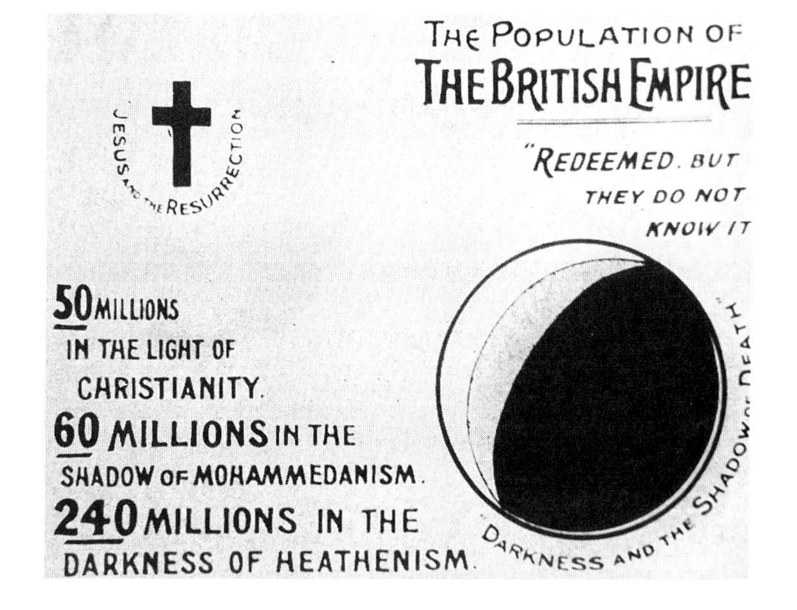

These supposedly frightening statistics were used to fuel the missionary fervour during Church Missionary Society lantern shows in the 1890s

'Bagishu Tribesmen', a Church Missionary Society lantern slide, c. 1885. Posed pictures of tribal battles taken by missionaries and sent back to Britain, reinforced the belief amongst the faithful of the need to civilize and Christianize Africa

used it not only to save souls but also to raise funds when supplies ran short. People flocked to watch the 'magic' of his lantern shows, often rewarding him with food.

Back in Britain the discovery of appalling poverty and degradation in the late Victorian city slums helped create a new breed of evangelical missionary who also made great use of the magic lantern. These were the zealous social explorers whose mission was to save the souls of those who inhabited the streets and drinking places of 'darkest London'. The people they encountered seemed to these missionaries to be as savage and as heathen as any tribe of Zulus or South Sea Islanders. One of the first to use the magic lantern to try to convert 'the lowest class' was Wilson Carlile, then a young preacher at St Paul's Church in North Kensington, London. In 1879 he began holding lantern shows for 'the rough lads of the district' in local schools. Carlile's biographer, A. E. Reffold, describes his method.

> Using the lantern he threw on the screen the most outrageously comic pictures he could get hold of and encouraged his audience to sing, clap, stamp and yell to their heart's content. This went on for about three quarters of an hour, until the fellows were exhausted – too hoarse to

shout, and with hands and feet too sore to applaud. Perhaps by this time it dawned upon the sharper of them that they had been badly fooled. At any rate, their rowdyism had been used as a weapon against themselves, for as soon as they were unable to make further sound, Wilson Carlile's turn came. He seized the opportunity to conduct what he called 'Family Prayers', a devotional conclusion to an evening not devoid of interest and excitement. While the 'Stations of the Cross', beautiful pictures in bas-relief, were thrown on the screen, a lady would sing a solo, usually 'There is a green hill far away'. When the picture of the Crucifixion was shown – a plain white marble Figure and Cross against a black background – a hushed silence fell upon the gathering. The roughest and hardest were won by this most simple and touching appeal to the heart, and the remarkable gatherings would often close with two or three strong, rough lads and men staying behind to kneel with Wilson Carlile and plead for strength to lead better lives.

Carlile went on to form the Church Army, an evangelical crusading wing of the Church of England which aimed to

The magic lantern became an effective device for teaching audiences about Christianity, both at home and overseas. When this kind of statuary was projected the intensity of light was such that the picture had enormous impact. Sometimes tints were used to make the statue change colour. The Victorians had a particular appreciation of sculpture and a great love of form

A Band of Hope slide of the 1880s, depicting a Christian soldier being guided through the jungle of temptation towards the Kingdom of God. Typically, the path of righteousness is represented by a stairway carved out of the ten commandments

On entering a church or chapel where a lantern service was being staged, the congregation would be confronted with this request for silence. Lanternists were very keen that their services should maintain a highly respectable tone

convert the poor by taking the message of salvation to them in the slums. The magic lantern was one of the movement's most powerful propaganda weapons. By the 1890s the lantern was also used by the Salvation Army and a host of other evangelical groups. Hundreds of horse-drawn magic lantern missionary vans trundled around Britain providing a platform for religious crusaders to save souls and attack the evils of drink and violence. One of these groups calling themselves 'The Good Templars' – who boasted more than 100,000 members in 1890 – claimed that 'the lantern is a feature which greatly rates among the villagers of all ages'.

The magic lantern was certainly a big crowd puller, especially in villages and rural areas where there were few entertainments. In South Wales, where the lantern was frequently used by revivalist preachers, it was common for pictures to be projected onto the outside wall of a church hall – for it would often not be big enough to hold the audience. And these religious pictures seem to have often had a deep impact on the curious onlookers. In an age before mass-produced picture books and before popular newspapers carried photographs, most poorer people were starved of visual imagery. For many the biblical scenes and symbols on the stained glass windows of the local church were the only religious images they had ever seen. Coloured lantern slides of the life of Christ and of Old Testament stories like David and Goliath would have had real dramatic power for some of these people. In the pages of local newspapers of the time we read of many a 'sinner' repenting and seeking forgiveness at a lantern crusade.

However, one should not overestimate the impact of the magic lantern at these evangelical gatherings. The memories of the few survivors who once peopled open-air lantern shows suggest that many saw them as free entertainment and not to be taken too seriously. Ted Harrison remembers the Church Army lantern shows of the 1900s.

> When we were hop picking in Kent, every year they'd put on one or two of these shows for us. It would be at night time when we'd finished work and we'd all crowd around, there must have been more than a hundred of us. It was great, there were funny pictures and views of places. If we hadn't had that we'd have just been sitting around the fire singing. Then there was the religious stuff at the end and some hymns. They thought they'd converted the bleedin'

> lot of us but there was no chance of that. We joined in with the hymns for a good sing song and we'd put dirty words in as well. It was a laugh really.

In early Victorian times, and for a hundred years before, the lantern was kept out of church and chapel services. Some more conservative churchmen would not even allow it in their buildings. Its associations with 'magic', children's treats and entertainment made it an unwelcome guest in the eyes of most church officials. However, in the late 1880s and 1890s there was a change of heart, probably inspired by the success of the evangelical lantern crusades. By the turn of the century many churches and chapels were holding lantern slide services. One leading lantern slide maker quoted in the magazine *TitBits*, in 1897, claimed that religious bodies were his main customers.

> We consider now, for instance, that no church or chapel is complete without a lantern. Until lately a magic lantern in connection with a religious service would have been looked upon by some I suppose as most objectionable; but now the demand for pictures of this character is such that we supply sets of slides for throwing upon the screen practically the whole of the Church Service both in English and Welsh. As for hymns, we have enough for a complete hymnal, nearly a thousand hymns in stock for this year's catalogue, and the number is constantly increasing. Then we have the chief incidents of the Bible from beginning to end. We find an increasing demand for this class of slides in our hire department. Sets are sent off on Friday night for the Sunday service, and returned to us on the Monday.

The actual task of setting up the lantern and using it in church was a complex one, and was the subject of much discussion and debate. Most lanternists projected onto a screen placed between the nave and the altar, and took great pains to ensure that the whole operation went smoothly. G. W. Nash writing in *The Optical Magic Lantern Journal* of 1894 gave advice on the methods he used.

> The screen should be hidden till required, and this will tax the ingenuity of the operator severely. Ours is an ordinary one, 20 ft square. It was so arranged that by a simple

A homestead in Uganda, c. 1885, pictured by an African missionary and used in Church Missionary Society lantern shows in Britain for the following twenty years

An unnamed missionary in Africa, c. 1895

movement or two, it flew into its place in a moment, having been out of sight during the first part of the service. It is done in this way. High up on either side of the chancel archway, on the choir side, pulleys are placed and cords passed through, and through the top hem of the screen. By these means the sheet is easily drawn and during service hangs behind one side of the archway, being fastened at the top and bottom on that side only. It is readily brought into place, and also withdrawn as readily by a choirboy. I might mention that the screen is hung high enough for the altar to be seen from beneath, as some people would object were it hidden. An electric buzzer or bell, with the gong removed, should have its push placed in the pulpit, so that the operator has notice when to change the picture. The

Church Army slide, c. 1890. In the evangelical revivalist movements of late Victorian times, magic lantern shows constantly repeated the message of original sin and the promise of personal redemption through faith in Christ

'The Wages of Sin', a Church Army slide of the 1890s, part of the Church's propaganda campaign attacking the 'evils' of drink and gambling. Their attempts to convert the poor – where most of their efforts were concentrated – were, however, largely unsuccessful

sounder, being close to the lantern, will not be heard by the congregation.

By the turn of the century more and more churchmen were regarding the magic lantern as essential to their ministry, for sometimes lantern services clearly had the power to stir the emotions of congregations. In 1902, for example, the *South Devon Journal* reported on the Good Friday lantern service of 'Christ's Divinity and Passion' at St Mary's Church in Torquay: 'so solemn and so soul inspiring was the whole of the service that many of the congregation were deeply affected by the dramatic and impressive relation of the Great Tragedy'. The novelty and impact of lantern services and lantern missions did not really fade until after the First World War.

CHAPTER NINE

YESTERDAY'S NEWS

Boy Scouts helping to keep crowd back

In 1852 the celebrated circus showman Lord George Sanger staged a magic lantern tour of the Midlands. It was his one and only venture in this area, which he later recalled in his autobiography *Seventy Years a Showman.*

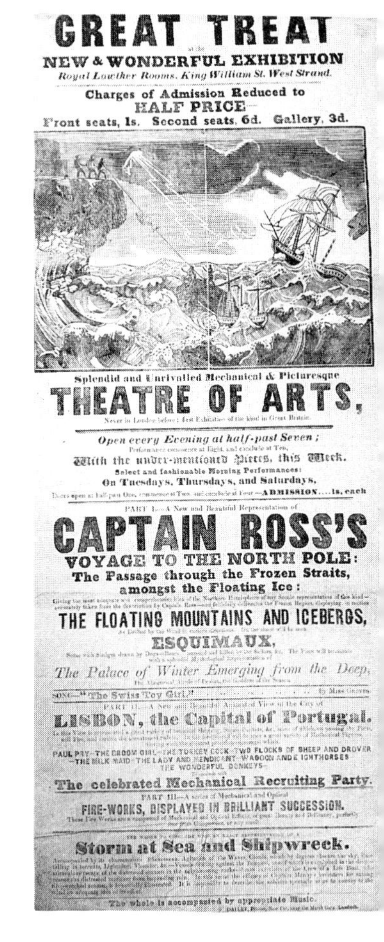

On 14th September the great Duke of Wellington died, and the magnificence of his obsequies was the talk of the land. I saw an opportunity in it for an exhibition that might prove very attractive in the winter months, during which I was now keeping out of London. So I arranged with a noted Sheffield firm of magic-lantern makers for two big lanterns and sixteen scenes of the duke's funeral procession, painted on glass, each plate being fifteen inches by four inches in size. These each threw a good picture on a white sheet some twenty feet square, and worked, one after the other slowly, had the effect of a large panorama. In addition to the funeral I had forty other slides, representing the search of Sir James Ross in the Arctic regions for Sir John Franklin. It was a subject much in favour with the people of that time, and with the story which I had off by heart and told as the pictures were displayed the entertainment was really a very attractive one.

The oxy-hydrogen or limelight for lantern purposes had then been introduced, so I had my lanterns fitted with the necessary apparatus and soon learned how to make the oxygen gas from a mixture of perchlorate of potash and other things that any local chemist could supply. When my preparations were complete I took various halls and rooms in the large towns of the Midlands for a winter tour.

It was not, however, to pass without a disaster. One night we were engaged in making the oxygen gas in the caravan in which we lived ready for an exhibition at the Town Hall, Northwich. The retort was upon the fire whilst I was busy with the curling-tongs to give my hair a graceful wave, and the grease-paint to put the necessary archness and colour into my face. Mrs Sanger was also getting into her finery in order to be ready to assist in working the show, and all seemed well. Suddenly there was a tremendous report, a blinding flash of light all around us, and the walls of our carriage which was our home flew to pieces. The retort had exploded. When we recovered we found that our injuries were very serious. My wife, who had been blown clean out of the end of the

Preceding page: *Young people in the news, assisting the forces of law and order. The youth movements of the late Victorian and Edwardian era were patriotic, uniformed and militaristic, contrasting starkly with the rebellious and individualistic youth cults of our own time. From the 1890s onwards, newsworthy lantern slides were often accompanied by short captions printed at the bottom of the photograph, to be read by audiences*

Left: *Poster for a lantern entertainment,* c. *1840. The main attraction is the voyage of Captain Ross, an arctic navigator who sailed in search of the lost explorer Sir John Franklin in the 1830s. His voyages seem to have remained newsworthy until the 1850s*

Above and right: *Lantern views of the Great Exhibition held in 1851 in the glass-domed Crystal Palace in Hyde Park. Sir Joseph Paxton's masterpiece covered 26 acres and housed 14,000 exhibitors. The exhibition was a showcase of scientific achievement, art and progress, celebrating Britain's position as 'the workshop of the world'. Six million visitors toured the exhibition, many of them arriving on excursion trains. Those who missed this spectacular event could enjoy it in lantern shows in their local village halls. The Great Exhibition remained a popular slide sequence for many years afterwards*

> caravan, was badly bruised, her hair singed off, and her face and arms much burned. My beautifully curled locks had disappeared with my light moustache and chin piece, my dress coat had fallen off me in tinder, while my hands and face were scorched to blackness. All that was left of the caravan was the floor and undercarriage. The rest was smithereens!

Exploding equipment was just one of the many problems facing the lanternist who aimed to show topical pictures and news events in the Victorian era. Communication was slow, the production of hand-painted slides was time-consuming, and photographic techniques were cumbersome. As a consequence, by the time the audience saw the pictures they were often yesterday's news.

In the early 1800s the centuries-old fairground peepshow – a box fitted with a small eyepiece – remained virtually the only medium through which ordinary people saw visual representations of newsworthy events. Paying the showman a halfpenny for the privilege, they peeped at crudely painted pictures of 'The Coronation of George IV', 'The Mutiny on The Bounty' and 'The Battle of Waterloo'. James Sanger, the father of Lord George Sanger, had one of the most spectacular fairground peepshows – it possessed twenty-six lenses so that twenty-six people could view at the same time.

The lanternists' first efforts to capture 'news' stories focused on the perennial favourites of popular literature – murder, war and disaster. However, the poverty of the itinerant lanternists made it difficult for them to keep their slides up to date. They could not afford to keep buying fresh supplies of topical slides and were loathe to throw away perfectly good though outdated ones. Consequently hand-painted slides like 'The Murder in the Red Barn' continued to be shown for twenty years after the events that they depicted. Some thrifty showmen got maximum mileage out of each slide by claiming that it represented whatever crime, war or disaster had just hit the headlines.

Sometimes early lantern shows would be sketched and painted by the lanternist himself. And in addition to displaying pictures of recent events and scenes, a few lanternists sketched the latest London fashions to try to lure the clothes-conscious woman into their audience. Even such modest attempts at topicality and newsworthiness could cause great excitement in small village communities. In 1894 Coriolanus

Moore writing in *The Optical Magic Lantern Journal* gave a vivid description of the first lantern show he had staged in his home village half a century before.

> In those days things moved slowly; a few carriers' carts, two or three times a week went to and from the country town some twelve miles distant, and were the chief means of keeping the place supplied with goods not produced in the immediate locality. A coach also ran through three times a week for the more expeditious passenger traffic, otherwise the sleepy old place jogged along with comparatively little contact with the outer world. Every Saturday the mail brought a supply of *The Weekly Advertiser*, containing full and fulsome accounts of local doings, and brief extracts from other papers, of how the world progressed in general. I need not say this paper was eagerly looked for and more eagerly read. It was, in fact, the sensation and excitement of the week. One issue contained the following announcement, printed in striking type, every other word beginning with a capital: 'An extraordinary lantern entertainment will be given in the National Schoolroom, Slowby Magna, in aid of the Slocum Sludge Almshouses, Nov. 4th, 18—, under the patronage of the nobility and gentry of the neighbourhood, by our well known and esteemed townsman, Mr Coriolanus D. Moore, who has received some marvellous moving pictures from London exhibiting changes of the most surprising character, and expounding Nature in a realistic manner hitherto unattempted. Mr C. D. Moore has also provided by his versatile pencil some sketches exceedingly interesting to the fair sex, of all the latest modes of millinery and dresses as worn at the present time by the aristocracy of London, in their varied colours and on life-size figures. Music and singing will be introduced at intervals by some of our best well-known local talent, who have kindly consented to assist. Afterwards a collection will be made in aid of the aforesaid deserving charity. The entertainment will commence at 7 o'clock and conclude with a grand realistic scene from the Sikh War, showing the destruction of a fortress, with some original effects. In anticipation of a large attendance, applications for tickets should be made at an early date.'
>
> I had secured the services of our curate, who had vast

> interest in the proceedings, to give a sort of introductory address before the lights were turned down and I prepared to show the first picture. The illuminated disc gleamed on the sheet and a brilliantly coloured 'Welcome' opened the show, wrong side up, but it was soon altered. A buzz of approbation, many long drawn out 'Ah's' and 'Oh's' when fizz, pop, out went the light, and we were, so to say, bathed in darkness. After a little time we started again, getting through about twenty pictures when there was a repetition of the fizzing and popping. The audience were very good natured and looked on this as part of the proceedings, till we again started with better luck, getting through most of the pictures before the costume slides were shown, which, I was informed, were eagerly anticipated by the female portion of the audience. The latest modes in bonnets and dresses on a life sized model caused raptures. The 'Oh's' and 'Ah's' were more plentiful than ever, with a running commentary . . . of the most animated nature.

It was not until the 1850s and 60s that lanternists began representing newsworthy events and scenes with any degree of

The wreck of The Bay of Panama *which crashed into the cliffs during a blizzard near Falmouth, Cornwall, on 10 March 1891. This was an epic shipwreck story made much of by lantern showmen for many years afterwards. Nine people, including the captain and his wife, were swept overboard by a great wave and drowned. Six other crew members froze to death in the night and the boatswain was said to have gone mad and jumped to his death in the sea. The survivors were taken to Falmouth in a horse-drawn omnibus, but this was caught in a snowdrift and its passengers had to finish their journey on foot, many of them shoeless*

The wreck of the Cunard liner SS Malta *which ran aground in thick fog near* Cape Cornwall *on 15 October 1889. She was bound from Liverpool to* Genoa *with a general cargo and nineteen passengers, all of whom were saved. More boats foundered off the coast of Cornwall in the days of sailing ships than on any comparable stretch of coastline in the world*

A railway accident in Burma in 1895. Sensational news events like rail disasters were featured in many lantern shows and late Victorian audiences were shown pictures of major accidents from the furthest corners of the Empire. However, pictures like this one would often not be seen until a couple of weeks after the event occurred

The Suffragettes' militant campaign for votes for women was characterized by daring stunts and protests, making the movement a photojournalist's dream. Their 'shocking' activities were – partly as a consequence – featured almost every week in lantern news slides from 1905 onwards. The captions were often extremely derisive and patronising towards the women involved

Whitehaven Colliery in Cumbria was often in the news in late Victorian and Edwardian times as it suffered a series of disasters, resulting in many fatalities, caused by gas leakages

authenticity and speed. This coincided with – and was heavily dependent upon – the artists and photographers who began to be employed by the popular press at this time. Some of the most spectacular and topical displays were usually at the Royal Polytechnic in London. A team of artists would produce finely detailed paintings based on engravings that appeared in *The Illustrated London News*. For example, in 1854 the Polytechnic staged an exhibition of dissolving views entitled 'The Russian War', including scenes of 'The Destruction of the Turkish Fleet at Sinope', 'Soldiers on the Danube in Winter' and 'The Flight from Nicopolis'.

Although most lantern shows remained weeks, months or even years behind the events they aimed to cover, they enjoyed a key advantage over the newspapers of the time: throughout the Victorian period newspapers did not have the technology to print the current affairs photographs they commissioned. The photographs were simply used as the basis for engravings and then discarded. The lantern, of course, could deal directly with the photographic image. So early war photographers like Roger Fenton who pictured the Crimean War in the 1850s often turned their photographs into lantern slides and reached big audiences in this way.

Similarly photographs of disasters at sea or rail crashes were also shown at lantern shows. Often they were much more stunning than the engravings which appeared in the newspapers. Shipwrecks, often pictured off the rocky Cornish coast where many ships foundered, were a favourite subject for lantern slides. From the 1880s onwards the lantern would never knowingly let a major disaster pass unrecorded. Sometimes notes would be published to accompany the 'bad news', often in the form of moralistic sermons and lamentable dirges. Like the Victorian press, the lantern producers romanticized calamity and liked to invest it with epic qualities.

The heyday of the lantern as a news medium came around the turn of the century. New photo agencies hired out the latest pictures to lanternists in theatres, music halls, and early cinemas. The photographs were a familiar fare of disasters, sporting triumphs and extraordinary events. Now they were often accompanied by short captions printed at the bottom of the photograph to be read by audiences. A new set could be ordered every week. So by the 1900s large audiences could, through the medium of the magic lantern, see life-size pictures of a news event only days after it happened.

Track and field athletics grew rapidly in popularity from the 1880s onwards. The driving force behind this explosion of interest was the army of public school and university educated men committed to physical fitness, sport and the ethos of 'muscular Christianity'

Wrestling was established as a popular working-class spectator sport by the 1890s. Contests were usually held indoors in halls, but Clapham Common provided one of the few venues for open air bouts

Events from the theatre and cinema world were often spotlighted by lantern news slides

Competitive winter sports, the most popular of which were ski-ing, tobogganing and the bobsleigh, were the latest fashion of the 1890s and 1900s. Women played a very important role in these early competitions and the organizations that staged them. When the St Moritz Bobsleigh Club was formed in 1897 it was stipulated that four-seater bobsleighs should have two men and two women in them for competitions. News pictures like this one, however, rather misleadingly created an impression of male dominance

The Oxford and Cambridge boat race was a major national event around the turn of the century which generated massive public interest – reflecting the domination of competitive sports by the public schools and universities. The first Oxford and Cambridge race was held in 1829 and it became an annual event from 1856 onwards

The rise of nationalism and the clashes between rival imperial empires which led to the First World War were graphically depicted in lantern news slides during the years before 1914

Floods and blizzards made good news pictures and so frequently appeared in lantern 'news' interludes

Smiling faces of East End children helping with the hop-picking in Kent. This was a regular photonews item to tug at the heart strings. The children would often wear their oldest clothes while working, then make a huge bonfire and burn them all on their last day in the hopfields. Their parents were able to buy them a new set of clothes with the money they had earned

CHAPTER TEN

RULE BRITANNIA

In November 1897 the magazine *Tit Bits* featured 'A Chat With A Lantern Slide Maker', a candid interview with one of Britain's major producers of lantern slides. When asked what the most popular contemporary events were for lantern coverage he replied confidently: 'war subjects, undoubtedly. I suppose nothing suits a lantern slide maker so well as a big war. We have not had a decent war – I mean from a lantern slide maker's point of view – since the Egyptian War. I got more money out of the Egyptian War than anything I ever did. Stanley's journey in search of Emin Pasha was also a popular subject.'

Military adventures were very popular with lantern audiences in Victorian Britain, with 'The Charge of The Light Brigade' and 'The Indian Mutiny' well-established favourites. But the appeal of imperialism went deeper and was more broad ranging than this. In 1897, the year Queen Victoria celebrated her Diamond Jubilee, the British Empire spanned about eleven million square miles and boasted a population of over 400 million, only 20 million of whom lived in Britain. This represented a quarter of the land mass of the world and over a quarter of its population. It was the largest empire in the history of the world, and the magic lantern faithfully mirrored the imperialism of the age.

There were many slide sequences with colonial themes like 'Fun Up The Ganges' and 'The Nigger and the Tigers' – often with strong racist overtones. The peoples of the Empire was another popular theme for lantern slides, in particular sequences on life in Africa, Australia, Canada and the South Sea Islands. India, the jewel in the crown of the Empire with its exotic settings, probably inspired more lantern sequences than any other country. It was through the lantern show that audiences in village halls all over Britain were able to picture the extent of the Empire 'on which the sun never set'. Some of the lanternists showed an early anthropological eye. Ernest Gedge, for example, of the Imperial British East African Company, took a series of photographs of remarkable clarity and vividness in what are now Kenya and Uganda.

The major imperial war that the lantern slide makers dreamed of came in 1898 in South Africa. The Boer War was to fuel a boom in magic lantern slides that would continue unabated for four years. It gave the lantern industry a golden opportunity to exploit the rising tide of jingoism and popular imperialism at the turn of the century. There was a flood of

Preceding page: *Part of the grand cavalcade which toured London in Queen Victoria's Diamond Jubilee celebrations in 1897. It was watched by 3 million spectators in the capital. On 22 June* The Times *wrote: 'Today the eyes of the whole Empire, and of millions of men beyond its pale, will be fixed upon London and upon the great and imposing ceremony in which we celebrate the sixty years of the Queen's reign'*

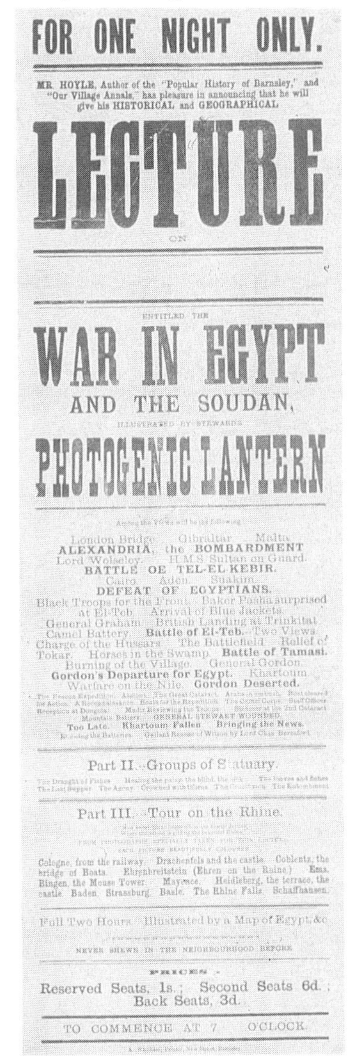

Poster for a lantern entertainment, promoting the work of Agnes Weston (1840–1918), a patriotic temperance campaigner who devoted her life to the moral reform of the Royal Navy. She formed many branches of the National Temperance League on board ships and opened a 'Sailor's Rest' in Devonport in 1879 offering 'Coffee, Comfort and Company'. The image of the British armed forces as being sober and morally upright formed an important part of the imperial dream of the late Victorian era

Left: *Poster,* c. *1887, advertising a lantern show featuring the war in Egypt and Sudan which had occurred two years before. General Gordon, who was killed in the siege of Khartoum, became the great imperial martyr of late Victorian Britain. Lantern shows like this one, held in village and church halls up and down the country, kept a heroic and idealistic image of him alive for the next ten years*

patriotic and propaganda slide sets with titles like 'Soldiers of the Queen', 'The Departure of the Yeomanry to South Africa' and 'Britons and Boers'. Some drew on the highly dramatized sketches which appeared in contemporary newspapers. There were even moving slides showing armoured trains with search-lights switching on and off, and shellbursts appearing and disappearing in a battle scene. Other sets used actors and actresses to pose as parting lovers embracing each other for the last time before the soldier went off to war. Melodramatic scenes like these were accompanied by specially written ballads or the hit song of the war — 'Goodbye Dolly Gray' – which

PART II.—Is a most beautiful Representation of the

SHRINE OF THE HOLY NATIVITY

At Bethlehem, the place where Jesus was born, showing the Manger and the place where the Magi worshipped him, with Midnight Mass, as performed on Feasts, &c.

Selections from the Masses by the Choir, with Organ Accompaniment.

A Grand Moving Diorama of INDIA, illustrative of the REBELLION of the SEPOYS, and

GREAT WAR IN INDIA!

ANIMATED WITH WONDERFUL MECHANICAL FIGURES.

1.—The commencement of the Mutiny at Merut, with the death of Colonel Finnis.
2.—Massacre of the British officers, their wives, and children, at Merut, with the Conflagration of the Officers' Bungalow.
3.—The Dragoon Guards in pursuit of the mutinous Sepoys on the Delhi Road.
4.—Hanging the Subahadar Major, the Chief of the rebels at Peshawur.
5.—March of the British forces towards Delhi.
6.—The fortress of Agra, and Palace of Akbar on the River.
7.—Interior of the Arsenal and Flagstaff Tower at Delhi, with the Explosion of the Powder Magazine.
8.—General Sir H. Barnard's attack on the mutineers in front of the Walls of Delhi.
9.—General Havelock's great victory over Nana Sahib.
10.—The City of Cawnpore, on the River Ganges.
11.—General View of the City of Delhi.

Grand Dioramic Change—THE BOMBARDMENT AND FALL OF DELHI.

The above represents the most startling and thrilling incidents which took place in India from the commencement of the Mutiny to the present time, and are illustrated by Grand Panoramic and Dioramic changes, in a series of views by first-rate Artists, from the most authentic Drawings. The brilliancy of the views—the intense interest awakened by witnessing a representation of the glorious victories of Havelock, the bombardment and conflagration of the far-famed City of Delhi, the City of Cawnpore (the scene of the atrocious murders), and the just retribution awarded to the mutinous Sepoys at Peshawur, together with other highly-interesting Views—make the above an object of interest, as it brings before the mind's eye those events which astonished Europe and showed the prowess of British Arms.

Doors open at Half-past 7, to commence at 8 o'clock.

Admission—A Few Reserved Seats, 1s.; Back Seats, 6d.

AFTERNOON PERFORMANCE at Five o'clock for Children. Admission 2d. each.

N. WALKER, General Printer, Charles Street, Briggate, Shipley.

Left, top: *Top of the bill on this poster advertising a magic lantern performance in 1860 is the Indian Mutiny of 1857. The crushing of the large rebel Bengal army by the outnumbered British troops was seen as a spectacular triumph. This 'little war' was re-enacted in lantern shows for the next thirty years or more, beginning with gruesome scenes of the massacre of the British officers and their families and ending with the Fall of Delhi*

Left, below: *Crowds cheer troops marching off to war in South Africa in 1899. This was one of many lantern sets produced on the Boer War – pictures of the conflict were in great demand among patriots back home. More than 5,000 British troops would be killed in the fighting, causing great public concern. The number of casualties however seems tiny compared to the millions who would be slaughtered during the Great War in the next decade*

audiences would sing along with. Most interesting of all, however, were the images of the troops marching through the streets, drilling on board ships and preparing for battle in South Africa. Here the lantern slides with their great clarity and sharpness of detail sometimes – perhaps inadvertently – began to capture the complex emotions of people at war.

Some of the most touching yet disturbing images captured by lanternists in the Edwardian era were of Empire Day celebrations. In the 1900s 24 May was designated 'Empire Day' and many schools staged patriotic plays and flag-waving processions for the children. The newly formed British Empire League provided schools with Union Jacks and councils paid for buns and souvenir mugs to encourage the children to join in wholeheartedly with the celebrations. Often there would be a magic lanternist in attendance too, photographing the children with a view to selling slides back to local schoolteachers and clergymen for their annual lantern 'shows' in which the children and their parents might pay a penny to see themselves on the screen.

Empire Day was just one of a number of imperial themes which provided a very lucrative market for the lanternist from

Celebrations among children in a Somerset village following The Relief of Mafeking in May 1900, marking a turning point in Britain's fortunes in the Boer War. In a spontaneous outburst of jingoism there were street parties, flag-waving processions and bonfires lit all over Britain to celebrate this event

A studio portrait of two young patriots taken in 1900. Children were often used to add pathos and sentimentality in imperialistic slide sequences where the inevitable message was duty to Queen and country country

Children celebrating the British 'victory' in the Boer war pose for a photograph in Bathford, Somerset, in the summer of 1902. Many of the children are wearing their 'victory' medals, issued by schools and churches

the 1890s onwards. There were more and more features on the might of Britain's battleships, reflecting the growth in international rivalry between the main imperial powers at this time. Portraits of life in the army and the navy also became extremely popular. In addition, many patriotic slide sequences also began to be produced for children. Some of the most popular lantern slide sets on sale at Gamage's around the turn of the century were 'British Battleships', 'Our Colonies' and 'The Illustrated History of The Union Jack'.

The monarchy had never been so popular as it was during the closing years of Queen Victoria's reign and there was a huge demand for up-to-date views of the royal residences and pictures of the most minor royal visits or ceremonial. Portraits of Kings and Queens had been a favourite since the days of hand-painted slides, but they increased greatly in popularity in the Victorian period. This boom in 'royal' lantern slides went in tandem with the emergence of spectacular imperial rituals and ceremonial occasions during the second half of the nineteenth century. The ritual celebrations of Victoria's Golden Jubilee in 1887 and the Diamond Jubilee festivities ten years later were recorded on hundreds of lantern slides which were shown for many years afterwards. And at this time when the British Empire was at its height, no magic lantern entertainment would have been complete unless it ended with a portrait of 'The Queen, God Bless Her', flanked by highly coloured flags.

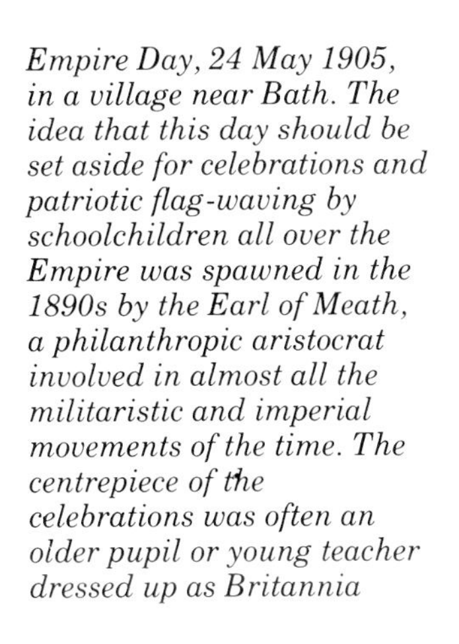

Empire Day, 24 May 1905, in a village near Bath. The idea that this day should be set aside for celebrations and patriotic flag-waving by schoolchildren all over the Empire was spawned in the 1890s by the Earl of Meath, a philanthropic aristocrat involved in almost all the militaristic and imperial movements of the time. The centrepiece of the celebrations was often an older pupil or young teacher dressed up as Britannia

One of the last portraits of Queen Victoria, dated 1900 when she was eighty. It was probably taken by James Valentine, one of the few photographers she allowed to picture her in her old age. Scribbled on the back of the lantern slide is the comment 'the fearful Boer War greatly troubled her'

Balmoral Castle, pictured in 1880 by George Washington Wilson, Photographer Royal for Scotland. Queen Victoria rarely visited Balmoral: her favourite residence, especially in her later years, was Osborne House on the Isle of Wight

Buckingham Palace, c. 1885. The slide inadvertently captures a window cleaner perched on a ladder at the second floor. During the late Victorian heyday of the British Empire there was a huge demand for up-to-date lantern views of the main royal residences

The Thanksgiving Service at St Paul's Cathedral formed the centrepiece of Queen Victoria's Diamond Jubilee celebrations in 1897. The Queen was now approaching eighty and very frail, so the service had to take place on the steps of St Paul's as she was too lame to climb them

EPILOGUE

In March 1896, G. R. Baker, a well-known magic lanternist, described seeing one of the first showings of the Lumière brothers' cinematograph at the Polytechnic in Regent Street, London.

> After a little introduction a picture appears on the screen, at the same time as the electric lights are turned out in the hall. What is it? It is a steamship pier, and there is a gangway in the mid-distance. A little whir is heard in the gallery above our heads, and the picture on the screen is all animation. Some one is walking up the gangway carrying a camera, and he is followed in quick succession by a hundred or so of others. Some turn to the left at the end of the gangway, and others to the right; every third or fourth person raises his hat as if he recognised someone that the audience cannot see; but when two or three run across the intervening space, one concludes that they wish to be quickly out of the field of view of the camera and that the salutations are for M. Lumière who is photographing this wonderful scene. The marvellous detail, even to the puffs of smoke from the cigarette, spoke volumes for the perfection of the apparatus employed . . . My advice to all lanternists is this, take the first opportunity to see the 'living photographs' I have described, and country readers should time themselves to be in Regent Street (Oxford Street end) five or ten minutes before any of the hours between two and ten p.m.

These 'living pictures', as they were then called, were the beginning of the end for the magic lantern. The new cinematograph, invented by the French brothers Auguste and Louis Lumière, quickly captured the imagination of the British public. It was the most sophisticated and successful of a host of late Victorian inventions – including the phenakistoscope, the zoopraxiscope, the kinetoscope, and, most important, the bioscope – which projected moving pictures. 'Living pictures' would in the following decades revolutionize mass entertainment, spawning a multi-million-pound film industry and creating the new habit of cinema-going, which was to be one of the most popular leisure activities of the twentieth century. The rise of the cinema was to eclipse the magic lantern and lead to its demise. In comparison to film, its static images seemed second rate and archaic.

Preceding page: *'Goodnight', a hand-painted slipping slide,* c. *1890, in which the master of ceremonies removes his hat at the end of the show. The rise of the cinema in the 1900s was to eclipse the magic lantern and lead to its demise. After the First World War once treasured lanterns and boxes of lantern slides became museum pieces locked away in cupboards and church halls*

However, the magic lantern did not disappear overnight. It remained important – though of secondary importance to film – throughout the Edwardian era, and continued to be used until the 1930s. The main reason the magic lantern held on for so long was because the film industry took a number of years to develop into its recognizably modern form. Hollywood did not begin its production until 1912. Film was not really taken seriously as an art form until after the First World War. And, most important, the first brick-built cinemas did not appear in British towns and cities until 1910, fourteen years after the introduction of the cinematograph. Before then cinemas were makeshift places converted from empty shops, mission halls or even coal cellars.

Most early moving picture shows were trundled around the country by professional showmen who put on their novel entertainments in music halls, assembly rooms and fairground booths. Sometimes these showmen were former lanternists now trying their hand at the latest fashion for film projection. During these early years the films were very primitive: they rarely ran for longer than two or three minutes; there were long delays during reel changes; and the projection equipment would frequently break down. To conceal these technical problems and whip up audience enthusiasm, the early cinema shows developed into a whole new art form in the fairground booths and circus tents. Interspersed between each film there would be clowns, magicians, circus turns, waxworks exhibitions or even boxing bouts. The emphasis in the film programme was usually on variety: there would be a few comedies, a couple of trick films and one or two news items. Magic lanterns would also be used as a stand-by in these variety shows, showing pictures of recent events, joke cartoons and illustrated song slides which the audience would be encouraged to sing along to. These shows proved immensely popular and the enthusiasm they generated provided the basis for the expansion of the film industry and permanent cinemas in Britain.

In the years before the First World War cinema-going became astonishingly popular, taking over from the music hall as the most favoured entertainment of the working classes. By 1914 there were forty-seven 'picture palaces' in Birmingham alone, that gave three afternoon shows and two every evening, and which together boasted a total seating capacity of 33,000. Even smaller centres like Salford, on the fringes of Manchester, had thirteen cinemas licensed under the Cinematograph

Act at this time. By 1917 the film industry in Britain was enjoying an audience of twenty million every week in about 4,500 cinemas.

The first kind of lantern slide to be hit by the cinema industry was the 'life model' melodrama of the type produced by Bamforth's. Melodramatic stories could be portrayed with much more power and realism in moving pictures, and this quickly became the most popular kind of film that audiences wanted to see. Around the turn of the century the new film-makers began to churn out one melodrama after another with titles like 'A Railway Collision', 'Fire' and 'The Jewel Thieves Outwitted'. Some used trick photography and special effects to heighten the sensational impact of their films. In 'A Railway Collision' (1898), for example, leading film-maker Robert Paul used toy trains to achieve the effect of a dramatic collision and engines plunging off the side of a mountain and into the abyss. Romances also quickly became very popular with titles like 'The Queen of Sheba' billed as 'the love romance of the most beautiful woman the world has ever known'.

To try to keep up with the times, Bamforth's turned briefly to film production in the 1900s, using the old magic lantern sets as film studios. They specialized in comic films for distribution in the North of England. And some of the old faces which appeared in the lantern slides graduated to celluloid. For example, the hero of Bamforth's slide set 'The Drunkard's Return' and his wife and child all appear in the film 'The Gypsy's Revenge'. Bamforth's, however, were to prove much more successful at postcard production.

Magic lantern news coverage, travelogues and documentaries were also quickly overshadowed by the new moving pictures. By 1901 cinematograph audiences could watch film of the Derby, the Boer War and the funeral of Queen Victoria. Brief and flickering though these news features were, the performance of the lantern appeared very inferior in comparison. Similarly, film-makers like Charles Pathé, whose French company dominated the early movie industry, also produced a host of travelogues and even a few documentaries, all of which were much more appealing to audiences than magic lantern pictures.

One added incentive for early cinematograph audiences was the chance to see local events or even themselves on the screen. Many of the showmen who ran the early cinemas and fairground bioscopes also doubled up as cameramen and directors, and they often produced 'phantom rides'. These were tracking shots usually taken from the front of a local omnibus or tram as it went down the High Street. The bus would be festooned with posters telling passers-by that if they went to the picture show they would see a glimpse of themselves on the screen. Local events like football matches, fetes, wakes weeks and Sunday School outings were also filmed out of similar motives. Magic lanternists had themselves used this ploy to increase their audiences in the 1880s and 90s, but they simply could not compete with the novelty of moving pictures.

The cinema, by winning over lantern audiences to the new medium of the moving image, also hit the advertising potential of the magic lantern show. From the 1900s onwards advertisers rapidly lost interest in selling themselves and their products through small-time lanternists and their one-off shows. The large picture palaces which sprouted up everywhere before the First World War were a far more attractive and profitable target for advertisers. One of the last major areas of advertising held on to by the magic lantern was the illustrated song promoting sheet music sales. However, by the end of the Great War the illustrated song craze had run its course. Sentimental ballads were now seen as old-fashioned, and magic lanternists found it difficult to illustrate the new up-tempo, jazz-influenced song and dance crazes. And the building of larger picture palaces with two projectors meant that there was less need for the singalongs which had once filled the long gaps while reels were changed.

The propaganda campaign waged by the Government during the First World War did give one short-term boost to the lantern trade. Slides imploring men to do their duty for King and Country were a regular feature of recruiting campaigns all over Britain. The lantern was also used to depict censored views of fighting at the front to audiences back home. However, by this stage the lantern had been largely superseded by newsreels and the cinema. These were the new media of communication and propaganda.

But the cinema did create one niche for lantern advertisements and propaganda which was to remain for many years. Most companies, apart from the big multi-nationals like Ford, found it difficult and expensive to make film advertisements. Instead they continued to produce lantern slides. Sometimes advertisements for well-known products would have a blank space where local merchants could insert their name and address. But the more enterprising local businesses would make their own slides to be shown in local cinemas. After the Second World War though, cinema advertisements became more more sophisticated, leading to the final demise of the lantern in this field. Nevertheless the basic principle of the magic lantern still survives in some cinema advertisements today – but now 'still' advertisements are shown on a colour slide projector, the modern successor of the lantern.

The cinematograph eclipsed the lantern not only as a public entertainment but also as a popular pastime at home. From the 1900s onwards home cinematography showing moving pictures began to displace the lantern from its proud place in the middle-class drawing-room. In 1900 even nursery film projectors could be bought. Increasingly the Christmas treat was to sit with father as he tried to master this latest piece of technology and put on a moving picture show. And a few more ambitious parents even started making their own home movies. Toy lanterns also lost their place as prized toys. They seemed more and more dated to children. Meccano – invented by Frank Hornby in 1901 – or the Hornby-Dublo train set became the most treasured Christmas presents for boys. By the 1930s, in an age of Hollywood movies and elaborate clockwork toys, the toy lantern was like a relic from a lost world.

Another major development around the turn of the century which greatly reduced the appeal of lantern slides was the reproduction of photographs in newspapers and magazines. This technical breakthrough, coupled with the emergence of a mass circulation popular press, meant that people no longer had to travel to a magic lantern show to see photographs. Now they simply flicked through the pages of their new *Daily Mirror* or *Daily Mail*. News and documentary photographs supplied by press agencies and the development of more sophisticated advertisements using photography all undermined former magic lantern strongholds. Bamforth's lantern factory in Holmfirth adapted to the reduction of demand for their slides with an ingenious switch in production. They geared themselves more and more to the mass production of cheap picture postcards – which were themselves made possible by the new printing methods. For Bamforth's the props, the studios and the hiring of child models remained much the same, but now the final product was not so much glass slides as glossy postcards in their millions. In some cases they simply lifted images from their old magic lantern melodramas, for example,